SMALL HOUSE
DESIGNS

Elegant, Architect-Designed Homes
34 Award-Winning Plans
1,250 Square Feet or Less

Edited by Kenneth R. Tremblay, Jr. & Lawrence Von Bamford

A STOREY PUBLISHING BOOK

Storey Communications, Inc.

This book is dedicated to our children,

Tamara and Rick
Cheyne and Kyle

The mission of Storey Communications is to serve our customers by publishing practical information that encourages personal independence in harmony with the environment.

Project edited by Elizabeth McHale and William Overstreet
Cover design by Meredith Maker
Cover photograph by Kenneth King
Text design and production by Mark Tomasi

The information in this book is true and complete to the best of our knowledge. All recommendations are made without guarantee on the part of the author or Storey Communications, Inc. The author and publisher disclaim any liability in connection with the use of this information. For additional information please contact Storey Communications, Inc., Schoolhouse Road, Pownal, Vermont 05261.

Storey Publishing books are available for special premium and promotional uses and for customized editions. For further information, please call the Custom Publishing Department at 1-800-793-9396.

Printed in Canada by Interglobe, Inc.
10 9 8 7 6 5 4 3 2 1

Library of Congress Cataloging-in-Publication Data

Small house designs / edited by Kenneth R. Tremblay, Jr. & Lawrence Von Bamford.
     p.   cm.
    "A Storey Publishing Book"
    ISBN 0-88266-854-4 (alk. paper). — ISBN 0-88266-966-4 (pbk. : alk. paper)
    1. Small houses—Designs and plans. 2. Small houses—Awards.
  I. Tremblay, Kenneth R. II. Bamford, Lawrence Von, 1937- .
  NA7126.S63 1997
  728'.37'0222—dc21
                                                               96-47252
                                                                    CIP

CONTENTS

PREFACE:
About the Competition

In 1995, Storey Communications sponsored an international competition to solicit small house designs from the global community of architects and designers. To announce the competition, the editors compiled a comprehensive listing of architecture and design addresses that comprised all 123 chapters of the American Institute of Architects (AIA), 87 builders identified with innovative housing designs, 83 international architecture and design organizations, 110 colleges of architecture from around the world, and 22 design-related journals and magazines published in North America, Europe, and Asia. All 425 organizations, schools, journals, magazines, and individuals received announcement letters. Additionally, the competition was posted via the Landscape Architecture Virtual Library located on the World Wide Web.

Five hundred fifty-two individuals and groups requested information regarding the competition. Each received by mail the call for entries, a list of factors to consider in designing small homes, and sketches of the types of drawings to be submitted. The program for the competition specified the following: design an elegant, environmentally friendly, energy-efficient, single-family home that is small only in physical size — not to exceed 1,250 square feet (excluding the garage or carport). It also directed the entrants to address both architecture and interior design. Minimum spatial requirements encompassed an entryway, a living room, a kitchen/dining area, two bedrooms with closets, one bathroom, laundry space, storage area(s), space for mechanical

systems, and an attached or detached garage or carport.

All competitors also had to submit the following:

- Statement of personal design philosophy
- Statement of design concept for the home
- Site plan (topography related to the footprint)
- Floor plan(s) with proposed furnishings
- Elevations (four) of the exterior
- Three-dimensional drawing (perspective) of the proposed exterior
- Comprehensive three-dimensional drawing (axonometric or section) of the proposed furnished interior
- Technical data for the home

Entrants proposed a total of 166 designs. To assist in evaluating the submissions, three outside judges were brought to Colorado State University in Fort Collins, Colorado: Jeffrey Cook, Regents Professor of Architecture, School of Architecture, Arizona State University; Elizabeth Wright Ingraham, granddaughter of Frank Lloyd Wright a practicing architect and an AIA Fellow, Elizabeth Wright Ingraham and Associates; and R. Craig Miller, curator of the Department of Architecture, Design and Graphics, the Denver Art Museum.

Entries were received from North America, South America, Europe, Africa, Asia, and Australia. The designers represented twenty-three countries, with the largest number of entries coming from the United States (sixty-five), Canada (seventeen), France (eleven), and Italy (ten). The majority of designers specified their own countries as the location of their planned houses. Most designed homes for areas requiring relatively high energy use — warmer humid climates or cooler humid climates.

Based on the final evaluation, Storey Communications selected thirty-four designs for this book, including the three prize-winning entries by Megan Williams (first), Hideyuki Takita (second), and Christophe Fayel (third). Together, these designs constitute a spectrum of practical, affordable, and environmentally friendly housing. In addition to the prize winners, the three out-side judges considered another twenty-one designs excellent based on their innovativeness and potential for the future. This latter group appears in a gallery of additional designs immediately following the Williams, Takita, and Fayel houses.

For the thirty-four principal designs, the editors allocated four or six pages to each, dictated by the materials received from the designers and the complexity of the design. Prices given for building cost and heating/cooling cost are estimates based on 1995 U.S. dollars and are location specific. For more information about a particular design, contact the appropriate architect; names and addresses appear at the rear of the book.

INTRODUCTION: Making Less into More

While some people continue to move into larger homes, others have begun opting for houses with less square footage. These smaller living units may be detached, site-built, single-family homes; manufactured homes; condominiums; apartments; or townhouses. They may be new, maintained as originally built, or remodeled.

For young families buying their first home or mature adults wanting to downscale, smaller houses make sense. Single adults or couples without children are also prime candidates for small homes. A vacation house for any size household might also be small.

Smaller spaces offer numerous advantages. They require less cleaning, painting, and routine maintenance. They also tend to be more easily negotiated by inhabitants and more energy efficient than larger homes. In addition, smaller homes may allow the owners more time to pursue recreational or other personal activities. Thus many individuals and families have discovered that small houses best meet their needs and lifestyles.

What Is Small?

The meaning of *small* isn't always clear; admittedly, it's a relative term. In the past, an average American home occupied 1,700–2,000 square feet. However, a great many of today's homes exceed 3,000 square feet. In the wealthy suburbs surrounding large cities around the world, houses of 10,000 square feet have become more common. Even these seem minuscule when compared to the palatial homes of Colorado, such as the former Good home in Denver at 33,000 square feet, and the new 55,000-square-foot home for a relative of King Faud of Saudi Arabia in Aspen. In contrast, the Japanese and many Europeans consider 1,000 square feet for a city residence to be quite generous. For this book, 1,250 square feet or less defines a small house.

A general misconception exists concerning small spaces and quality. To some people, small connotes cheap or less desirable. However, to quote a familiar saying of the internationally acclaimed architect Mies van der Rohe, "Less is more." Small spaces in fact can be jewel-like, ideal places for living. The question is, how can a design either create or re-create qualitative space that, although limited in square footage (reality), looks larger and roomier than it actually is (illusion)? Certainly craftsmanship and materials are decisive factors. Craftsmanship should be the best the owner can afford; after all, almost anyone can recognize superior craftsmanship, which should be regarded as a long-range investment. Selecting quality materials — for example, marble, slate, exotic woods, copper, stainless steel, and glass — will also help make the home a statement of personal values and taste.

Combining expensive and ordinary materials can make the project affordable without compromising quality. The Viennese archi-

1

tect and Pritzker Prize laureate Hans Hollein commonly integrates costly materials with everyday ones. In the same interior he will use real marble, a painted-on impression of marble, and a Formica marble laminate. Thus with careful planning, sophisticated small homes can be built without spending a fortune.

Key Design Elements

To achieve optimum results, small spaces must be transformed through the act of design. The key is to create what may be termed illusionary space — that is, space that appears to be more extensive and desirable than what actually exists. Small spaces should make living easier, more cost efficient, and more enjoyable.

The design elements listed in the adjacent box can be marshaled in many ways. For example, mirrors can essentially double space, photographic murals can provide a three-dimensional perspective, and built-in furniture and storage walls can free up floor area. People perceive a rectangular space as larger than a square space of the same square footage. Where white walls ordinarily move backward visually, in some situations appropriate lighting can make combinations of dark and light colors equally effective.

Any design device that distracts the viewer from noticing the intersection of planes or the termination of features provides the illusion of a continuum. Visual variety in interiors, especially where the geometry of the interior architecture (the six planes of an enclosure) is concerned, adds to the illusion of enhanced space. Proportion and scale become very important; choosing smaller-scale objects and furnishings will suggest to the eye that the interior space is larger than it in fact is.

The following elements can visually and functionally enhance a small house:

- *Glass on the perimeter*
- *Skylights*
- *Mirrored walls*
- *Glass-block walls*
- *Curved walls*
- *Angled wall planes*
- *White or neutral walls*
- *Wall photo murals (in perspective)*
- *Single-pattern floor coverings*
- *Wall-to-wall floor coverings*
- *Large furnishings against walls*
- *Multiple activity rooms*
- *Open traffic patterns*
- *Multiple-purpose furnishings*
- *Horizontal wall graphics*
- *Soft surfaces*
- *Glass tabletops*
- *One-story floor plan with variety*
- *Appropriate human scale*
- *Smaller-scale furniture and artworks*
- *Built-in furniture and storage walls*
- *Small-scale floor/ceiling tiles*
- *Linear floor lines*
- *High ceilings*
- *Next-to-ceiling shelving*
- *Lighter-color furnishings*
- *Rounded corners*
- *Colors in corners*
- *Spotlights on selected objects*
- *Pocket doors*
- *Transparent/translucent screens*
- *Core functional areas*
- *Simple and precise arrangements*

With regard to wall colors, the same light hues should be used throughout the dwelling for visual continuity and for their space-expanding qualities. Cool hues may be blended into an atmospheric perspective, thereby creating the illusion of greater depth. Lighting small interior spaces through indirect lighting, wall washing, and accent illumination also visually expands boundaries. Detailing can make the difference between a nice home and a dignified residence. Architectural elements, handles, hardware, and fixtures can all contribute. Several custom-designed elements, such as the entrance door, can transform the entire image of the house.

A smooth transition between the exterior and the interior will appear to bring the environment inside, thereby further expanding visual space. Glass doors, windows, and interior plants help to create the desired illusion. Thus a combination of innovative interior and exterior design can produce a dynamic, non-claustrophobic atmosphere.

Environmentally Conscious Homes

Frank Lloyd Wright extolled the beauty of nature, insisting that his houses grow from and work in harmony with their surroundings. Wright knew that home environments affect physical and psychological well-being. With the burgeoning global "green" movement, more homeowners, builders, architects, and designers are adopting Wright's philosophy. The emerging goal is to create environmentally conscious homes that remain functional and aesthetically pleasing.

A growing number of designers are following a holistic approach, one that includes solar orientation, daylighting, healthy ventilation systems, and environmentally friendly components, such as recycled materials and energy-efficient windows. Characteristics that help define an environmentally conscious house include energy conservation, eco-lighting, recycling and waste reduction, superior air quality, toxin reduction, and environmental integration.

Energy Conservation

Conserving energy ranks as a top priority. In northern climates, site selection should typically direct the most prominent openings and views toward the south. A cluster of large windows on the south side of the home takes advantage of passive solar heat gain and allows occupants to connect with the surrounding environment. High-quality insulation is crucial for energy efficiency: R-19 for walls and R-38 for the roof in colder climates. Caulking around windows, doorjambs, and gaps in home siding is also important, with preference given to water-based caulking. Evergreen trees and bushes planted on the north and northwest of the home will act as a windbreak for winter winds, while deciduous trees to the southeast and southwest will block the sun during the summer but let it shine in during the winter months.

Appliances and other electrical equipment are now being designed with an eye toward both energy efficiency and a healthy environment. American homeowners can make intelligent, energy-efficient appliance choices by studying the yellow EnergyGuide labels when shopping. For example, new high-efficiency refrigerators use about half as much energy as older models. Consumers can also find heating systems that are 94 percent energy efficient and provide both home heating and virtually unlimited hot water. For cooling, evaporative coolers work well for hot, dry homes while using only 30 percent of the energy of an air conditioner.

Low-cost and easy methods to cut energy consumption include installing a programmable thermostat and regularly tuning heating and cooling systems. Environmentally friendly personal computers have been introduced that automatically reduce their energy consumption when idle. More-expensive conservation measures include adding a solar collector or wind system to produce electricity on site.

Eco-Lighting

Windows, skylights, and glass doors should be planned to allow generous amounts of natural light to penetrate the home's interior. The best eco-lighting makes the most of indirect daylight. Outside controls, such as awnings, overhangs, and trees, help to shade or deflect direct light from the sun, which can fade furnishings and dry out leather. Currently very popular, double-cell shades and pleated shades with metalized backing come in soft designer colors. Draperies can provide a complete blackout or just about any degree of light transmission desired. An interior designer might consider using pale shades to reflect light, combined with darker-colored draperies for aesthetic contrast.

Given the abundance of windows in most green homes, homeowners should ensure that all windows are energy efficient. Fortunately, a variety of thermally efficient windows are now available, often featuring double- or triple-sealed panes filled with inert gas and a low-E coating to reduce heat transfer. Artificial lighting should also be energy efficient and planned specifically to meet the homeowner's needs. Compact fluorescent (CF) bulbs are often a good selection. They can typically be inserted into incandescent sockets, where they last up to five years and use 75 percent less energy than incandescent bulbs. Another efficient lighting possibility is the halogen bulb, which uses 30 percent less energy than an incandescent bulb. Other ways to improve lighting efficiency include:

- Using lighting only in spaces where activity requires it

- Keeping lamps clean
- Decorating with paler hues and tones on walls and ceilings to increase usable light
- Installing a rheostat or dimmer switch to adjust wattage flow as needed (however, you cannot use a rheostat with CF lighting)
- Employing timers, photocells, or occupancy sensors to switch off unnecessary lights

Recycling and Waste Reduction

By now most people have been exposed to the three Rs: *reduce* the amount of waste, *reuse* products whenever possible, and *recycle* as many products as possible. Following these three Rs is essential to living in an environmentally conscious house.

To facilitate waste separation, a homeowner can sort and store everything in one spot. A recycling station near the kitchen door or a door leading to the garage minimizes effort when removing waste from the house. Many inexpensive products are now available to equip a recycling station, including molded plastic containers sold by discount stores.

Recyclable products can be used throughout the home. Examples are:

- Floor tiles made of recycled glass
- Interior panels made of recycled newsprint and covered with fabric
- Eco-furniture made of previously used wood, plastic, or paper
- Wallpaper made of recycled paper and wood chips
- Carpet made of recycled plastic

In redesign, existing components of a house can be reused, fixed, updated, or reworked rather than thrown away.

Water conservation can significantly reduce waste. U.S. residents use an average of 70 gallons of water a day, mostly in the bathroom; a family of four uses 100 gallons for toilet flushing and 80 gallons for bathing and showering. Switching to a low-flow toilet, which consumes only 1.6 gallons per flush, is the most important change. A low-flow showerhead also conserves water. Showerheads are now available that use only 2.5 gallons per minute while still providing good spray patterns. Switching to a water-conserving dishwasher can save over 1,500 gallons of water a year. Other possibilities include:

- Adding faucet aerators, which slow water flow to 2 gallons per minute
- Switching to a front-loading washing machine, which uses 33 percent less water than a top-loading machine
- Using trickle irrigation and timed water sprinklers to water drought-tolerant landscaping
- Capturing rainwater to meet some water needs

Quality Air

Environmentally conscious houses must be well ventilated to maintain a high level of air quality. Indoor air pollution — that is, harmful gases or particles released into the air — has two major sources: the building itself and the occupants. A surprising study conducted by the U.S. Environmental Protection Agency (EPA) found that indoor levels for eleven air pollutants were two to five times higher than outdoor levels.

The best way to control indoor air quality is through proper ventilation, and especially adequate air exchanges. Air will flow naturally by simply opening windows in the home. The most desirable system allows air to enter through small, low-level openings on the windward side and then exit on the other side via clerestory windows or skylights. Exhaust vents in the kitchen and bathroom provide localized ventilation.

Homeowners also need to make sure that the attic is well ventilated — vents set high in the ridge and low in the soffits are the most effective combination for comfort and efficiency. A very efficient whole-house attic fan can be used for bringing in fresh air in warm weather. An air-to-air heat exchanger is an efficient way to keep air clean during cold weather.

Plants help maintain clean air by acting as natural filters. The Foliage for Clean Air Council recommends one potted plant per 100 square feet. The green spider plant, golden pothos, and philodendron appear especially effective.

Other suggestions to control indoor air quality include:

- Eliminating smoking in the home
- Humidifying the air with large bowls of water or commercial humidifiers
- Checking gas and flue pipes to ensure that they vent outdoors
- Selecting interior finishes, such as hardwoods and metals, that do not produce or retain dust
- Limiting open shelving space to prevent dust accumulation

Toxin Reduction

Exposure to toxic chemicals in the home can aggravate symptoms of allergies and compromise the immune system to the point where disabling sensitivities to certain chemicals can develop. Such chemical hypersensitivity affects an estimated 15 percent of the American population.

To remove toxins, a homeowner can begin by substituting natural products for aerosol sprays, moth balls, and air fresheners. Switching to environmentally safe cleaning products, such as citrus-based solvents, also helps. Carpeting and area rugs should be vacuumed at least once a week, perhaps with a central vacuum system that vents particles outside the house.

A homeowner should also minimize volatile organic compounds (VOCs) in the home. These are essentially fumes and vapors associated with almost any manmade product — for example, adhesives and carpeting — especially in a confined space. Healthy substitutes are available. Natural fibers, such as cotton, wool, linen, and silk, are typically better than synthetic materials. When selecting paint, consider using zero-VOC latex types, which many specialty paint stores now carry. When installing tile floors, select the new epoxy-based grouts that seal permanently. When buying new carpeting, American consumers should check to see if it has the Carpet and Rug Institute's Indoor Air Quality label. Such carpets contain low VOC levels and can be secured by a new environmentally friendly Velcro system.

More-serious toxins in the home include lead, asbestos, formaldehyde, carbon monoxide, and radon. Several kits are available to test for the presence of such toxins. If building a new home, talk to the builder. To remove specific toxins from an existing home, contact a mitigation professional.

Electromagnetic fields (EMFs) also concern some homeowners. Reducing the number of electrical appliances in the home and keeping a distance from operating electrical devices can lower EMF exposure.

Environmental Integration

The "Wrightian formula" integrates the house with the surrounding landscape. Windows provide a view to nature, mirrors can reflect the outdoors, plants inside can complement outside plants, and a lawn

chair placed inside brings the garden indoors. Placing fresh flowers and easy-care plants throughout the house creates an aesthetic as well as a healthier environment.

Decorative schemes can reinforce the environmental theme. A mural of an outdoor scene, dinnerware with flower prints, and artwork depicting nature are three possibilities. Another is the use of wallcoverings with environmental patterns, such as fruit, herbs, animals, leaves, and stones. An appropriate color palette might include golds, oranges, and greens. Matte finishes and nature neutrals of white, beige, sand, and terra-cotta also suit many of today's environmentally conscious houses. Used both inside and outside, such natural materials as wood and stone enhance the green home concept.

Conclusion: The Small, Environmentally Conscious Home

In the future, because of cost, resource limitations, and personal choice, an increasing number of individuals and families will probably live in small houses. As the designs included here amply demonstrate, such small living accommodations can be just as elegant and enjoyable as any other, and just as valid an expression of personal style.

Moreover, small homes, whether new or refurbished, can readily integrate the principles of environmental design. A small, environmentally conscious home not only helps preserve our natural resources, but also offers long-term cost savings and a potentially cleaner, healthier milieu.

This book is dedicated to helping homeowners achieve these ends.

THE HOUSE DESIGNS

Perspective

HOLLOWAY

Jury Comments

An exciting design where Scottish, English, and Italian concepts all come together to form an architectural synthesis. A number of ingenious features prevail, such as the stairway tower, organically curved wall, and sensitivity to available light. The house is reminiscent of fortified Scottish manor houses.

The objective of this design is to create a strong house that incorporates both modern and traditional elements, and that introduces novelties where possible to maximize aesthetics and utility. The ideal occupants would desire an imaginative spatial layout, despite modest means.

The central design concept is a wall that spirals, evolving like a seashell and forming an organic sequence of three spaces that repeats on the two upper levels. Kitchen and bathroom services occupy the central core, which opens to form the dining room (ground floor), bedrooms (first and second floors), and finally the primary space — a double-height living room. The living room opens onto the garden terrace and is oriented for passive solar gain, with a curtain wall facing south. An insulated solid wall to the north minimizes heat loss.

Even though small, the house is not a minimum-standards dwelling. Technologically innovative in its details, the design emphasizes the latest solar and environmental technologies while still being practical to construct. Photovoltaic silicon-cell panels on the roof provide for all the energy needs of the house.

Nigel A. Holloway

Technical Data

Gross Square Feet:
1,050

Location:
England; any suburban or semirural site

Type:
Brick detached
private dwelling

Materials:
White rendered-brick insulated cavity walls, concrete foundations and floor slabs, wood, ceramic tiling, stone paving

Estimated Cost to Build:
$130,000

Estimated Cost to Heat/Cool:
$0

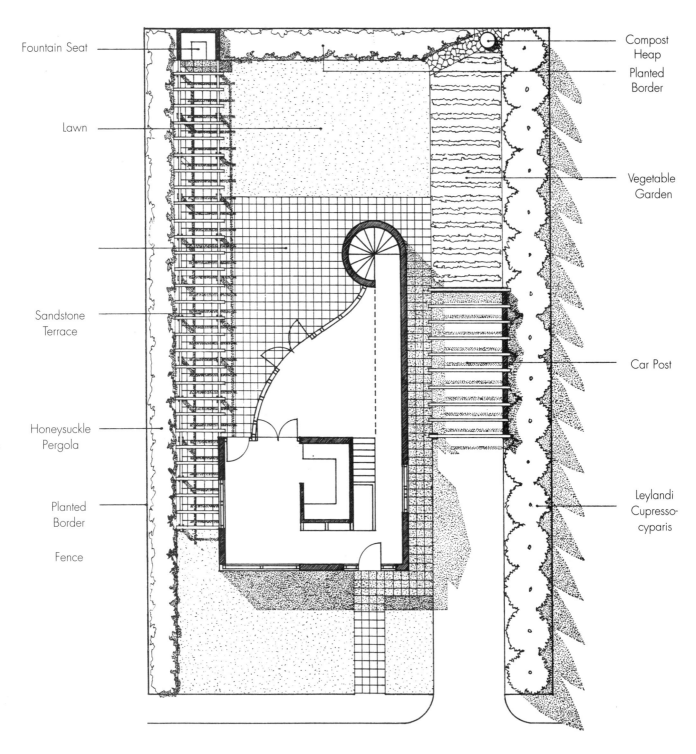

Fountain Seat

Lawn

Sandstone
Terrace

Honeysuckle
Pergola

Planted
Border

Fence

Compost
Heap

Planted
Border

Vegetable
Garden

Car Post

Leylandi
Cupresso-
cyparis

Site Plan

Floor Plans

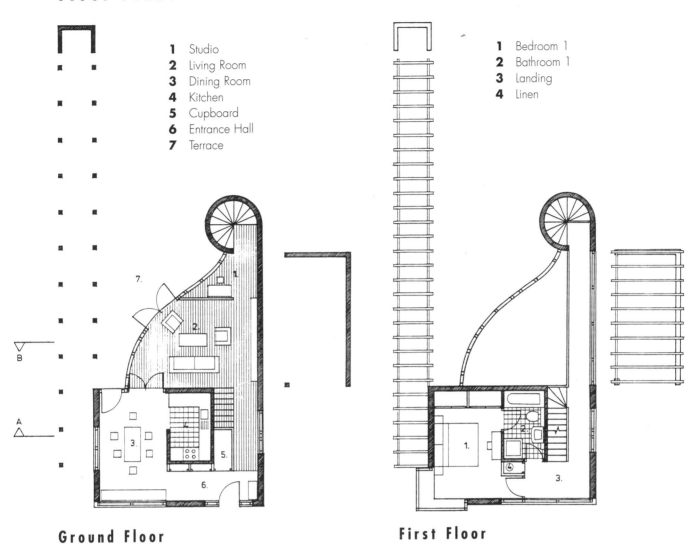

Ground Floor

1 Studio
2 Living Room
3 Dining Room
4 Kitchen
5 Cupboard
6 Entrance Hall
7 Terrace

First Floor

1 Bedroom 1
2 Bathroom 1
3 Landing
4 Linen

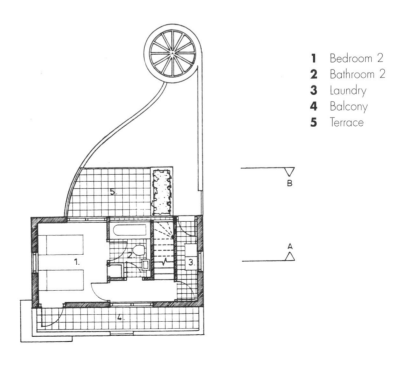

Second Floor

1 Bedroom 2
2 Bathroom 2
3 Laundry
4 Balcony
5 Terrace

11

Elevations

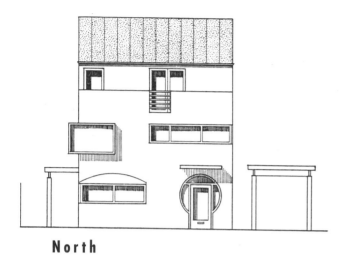

North

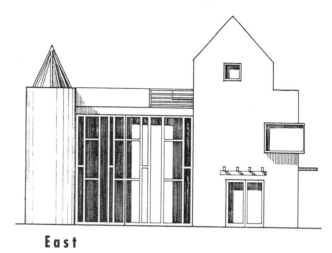

East

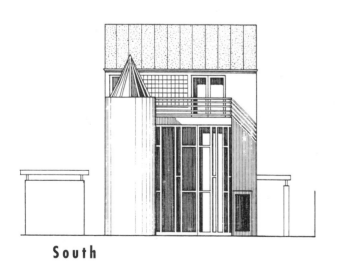

South

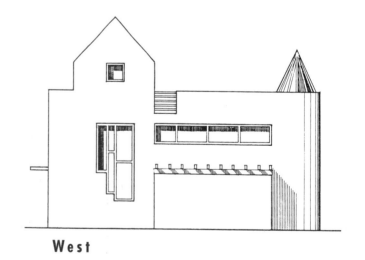

West

Axonometrics

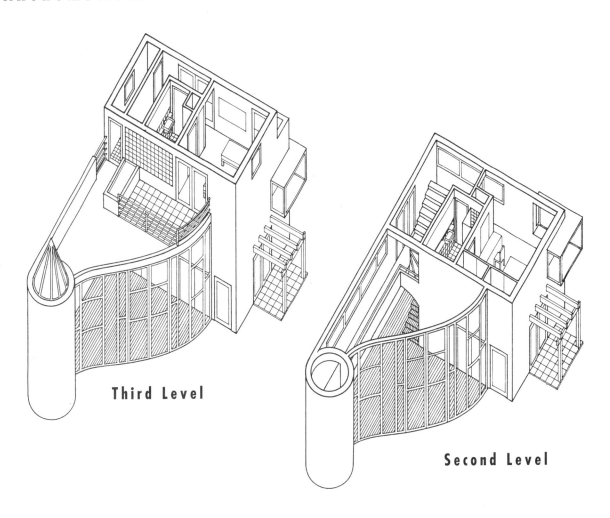

Third Level

Second Level

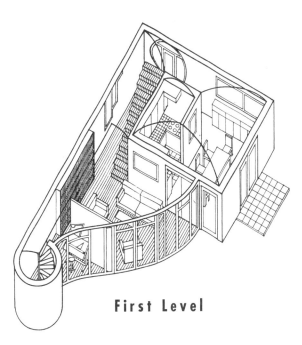

First Level

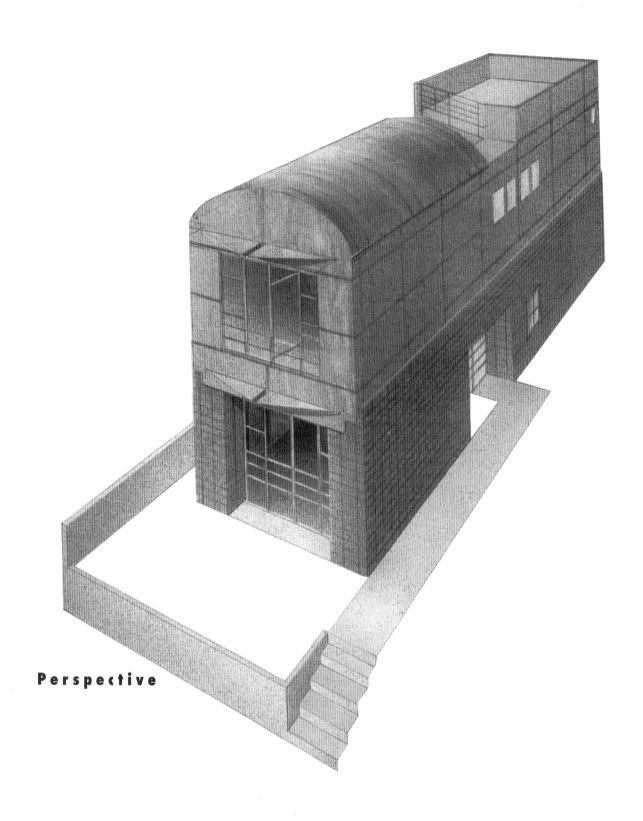

Perspective

FOLONIS

Jury Comments

This elongated, two-story house contains several unique features, including an upper deck that separates the study and master bedroom. The exterior has a subtle postmodern typology.

Is the built environment a reflection of our society, regionalism, or both? Is there such a thing as architecture that reflects culture or makes a social statement about a particular region? I present a position that, first of all, takes a philosophical view of the practice of architecture in Los Angeles and, second, determines how to make architecture in that context.

The region has grown and evolved under the influence of Hollywood, which, since its inception, has focused on creating temporary objects of illusion. I believe that architecture needs to be marked by a higher level of permanence and craft to be of lasting value and to contribute to our culture.

Public spaces, including entry, living, dining, kitchen, and water closet, occupy the first floor. Private living spaces, including three bedrooms, two bathrooms, and a study, fill the second floor, which is broken into two areas separated by an exterior deck and linked by an interior hall.

The house achieves energy efficiency through its southwest orientation and its building materials. The first floor does quite well with the exposed concrete floors and walls. During the extreme cold days in the winter, the residence uses very little mechanical heating to maintain a temperature of 68 degrees Fahrenheit. Conversely, the extremely hot days in the summer require almost no mechanical cooling, as cross-ventilation cools the house naturally. The canopy on the front elevation provides sufficient sunscreening to the southwest-facing elevation during the summer solstice. The roof area over the children's bedrooms serves as a rooftop garden.

Michael W. Folonis

Technical Data

Gross Square Feet:
1,200

Location:
Santa Monica, California

Type:
Wood frame, concrete blocks

Materials:
Polished concrete slab, exposed concrete blocks, mahogany plywood, gypsum wallboard, copper roof

Estimated Cost to Build:
$72,000

Estimated Cost to Heat/Cool:
$500 per year

Floor Plans

1 Entry
2 Living/Dining Room
3 Kitchen
4 Breakfast Area
5 Water Closet
6 Garage
7 Stairway
8 Master Bedroom
9 Bathroom
10 Bedroom
11 Closet
12 Study
13 Deck
14 Stairway to Deck
15 Landscape Area

Lower Floor

Upper Floor

Elevations

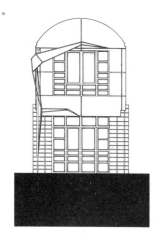

South

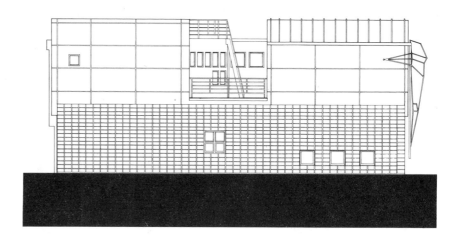

East

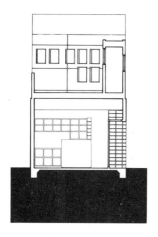

North

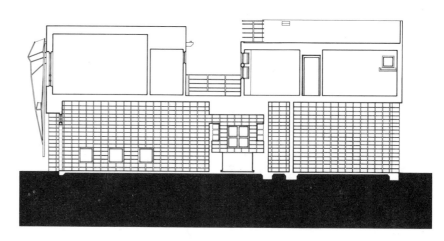

West

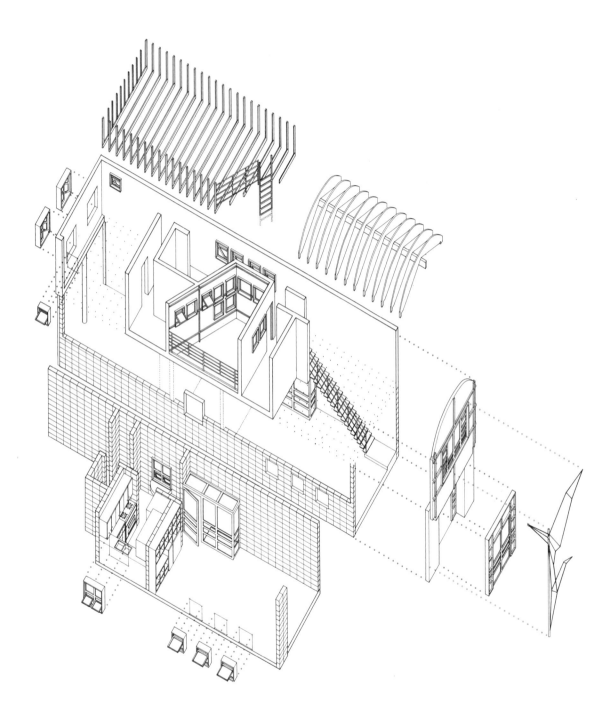

Exploded View

Perspective

AKKURT & AKKURT

■ Jury Comments

A great open plan featuring wide traffic patterns and a curved staircase. The home has a rather formal arrangement, but with a logical interrelationship of functional components. This design reflects order, and derives from the architectural heritage of New England.

Located in a Massachusetts college town, this two-story home nestles among old lilacs, maple and black walnut trees, and evergreens. The design effectively uses passive solar heating and cooling. To achieve maximum efficiency it features a southern orientation with a minimum fenestration on the north. In the winter, solar energy is collected directly through the two-story solarium and south windows. Coniferous trees in the north act as buffers, helping to block winter storms, wind, and snow. In the summer, deciduous trees on the south side interrupt the flow of solar energy before it strikes the ground, windows, and wall surfaces. Designed as recessed areas, both bedrooms benefit from shading created by the solarium's overhanging roof. The bay window performs a similar function for the living room.

Articulation of the facade openings directly responds to the orientation and the quality of light, with the recessed deck on the south and the bedroom windows on the north. This allows an abundance of natural daylight into the private and public spaces. Operable awning window vents high above the solarium glazing, doors, and all windows contribute to natural cross-ventilation. For cooling, the vents of the solarium and the doors to the deck permit thermosiphoning.

The first floor consists of public or shared areas. The second includes a master bedroom that enjoys a private deck, another bedroom that opens below to the solarium, and a full bathroom connected to laundry space. All living areas downstairs and the bedrooms upstairs share the south view.

Hasan Akkurt and Cigdem T. Akkurt

■ Technical Data

Gross Square Feet:
1,230

Location:
Northampton, Massachusetts

Type:
Wood frame construction on concrete slab

Materials:
Painted wood clapboards, foiled-back batt insulation, gypsum wallboard, asphalt shingle roof, ceramic tiles, maple strip flooring, aluminum windows and door frames

Estimated Cost to Build:
$79,950

Estimated Cost to Heat/Cool:
$800 per year

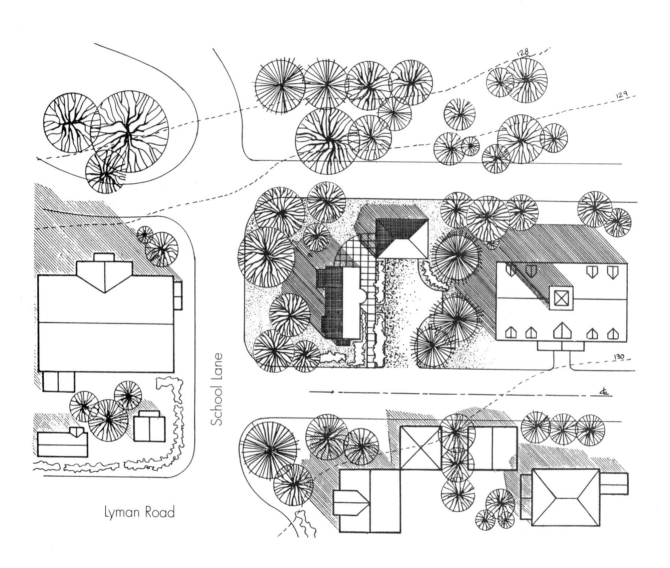

School Lane

Lyman Road

Site Plan

Floor Plans

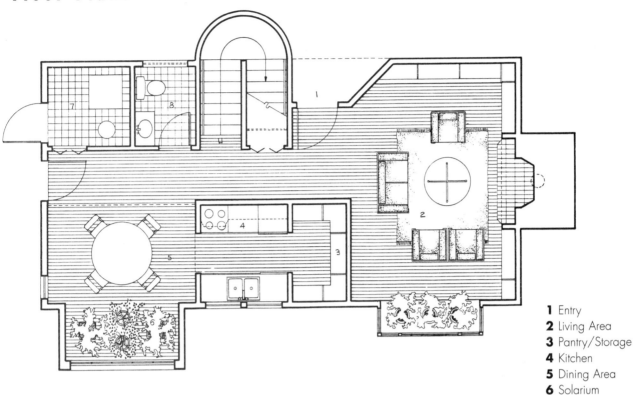

First Floor

1 Entry
2 Living Area
3 Pantry/Storage
4 Kitchen
5 Dining Area
6 Solarium
7 Mechanical Room
8 Toilet

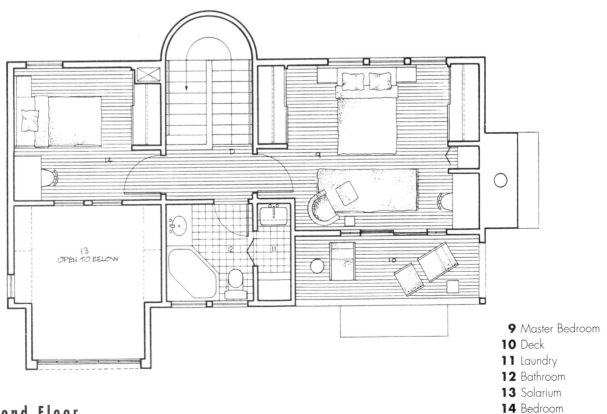

Second Floor

9 Master Bedroom
10 Deck
11 Laundry
12 Bathroom
13 Solarium
14 Bedroom

Elevations

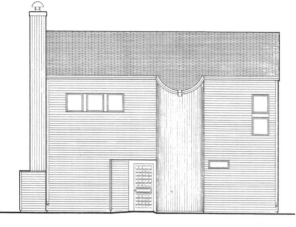

North

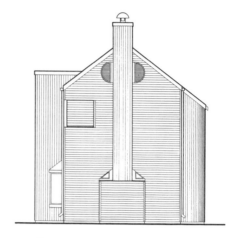

East

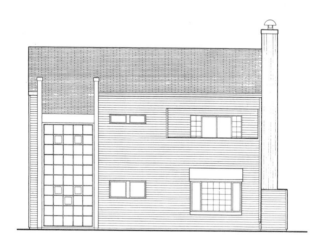

South

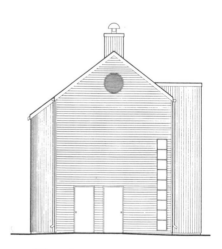

West

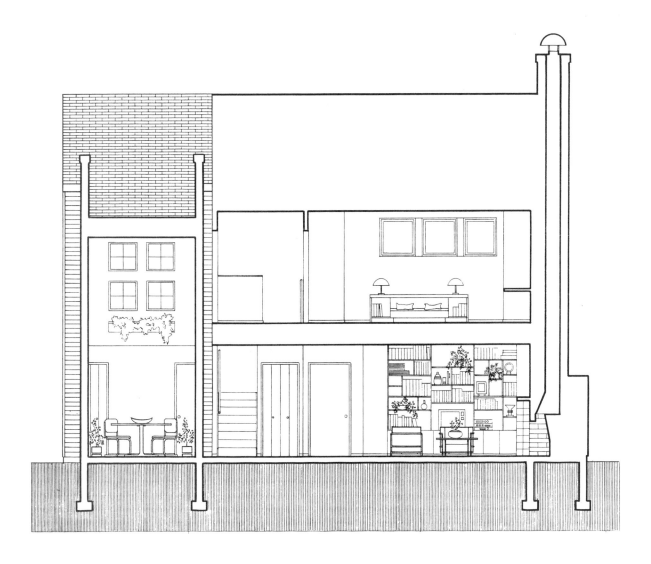

C u t a w a y

Perspective

REED AXELROD ARCHITECTS

The decking, a porch, and a separate garage contribute to the illusion that this home is larger than it actually is. The house would settle nicely into a variety of neighborhoods.

We designed this affordable home as a prototype for the Northeast Winston Redevelopment Area in Winston-Salem, North Carolina. The area features small frame bungalows and clapboard farmhouse-style duplexes ranging from forty to seventy years old. The house and garage form components of an extended L-shaped plan. Depending on site conditions, the pieces can be rotated or reflected to provide different arrangements.

By balancing public and private zones, sun and shade, curb appeal, outdoor spaces that expand the rooms, and indoor-outdoor circulation sequences, this design constitutes a thoughtful addition to the neighborhood fabric. Styled in a manner that appeals to prospective first-time home buyers, it relates well to neighboring houses and is conventionally constructed. An appropriate level of construction technology permits the home-owner to make repairs, additions, and modifications with materials found at commercial home centers.

The floor plan emphasizes flexibility. First and second floors are each 590 net square feet, with communal spaces below and equally proportioned bedrooms with bath above. A partial basement provides room for storage and mechanical services.

Mechanical equipment is located in the attic, with access by a folding stair above the second-floor hall. The attic provides additional storage space with excellent thermal insulation from solar heat gain. The garage is unfinished but adaptable to many uses, and the loft, with dormers, can serve as a rental apartment, office, or guest room.

Reed M. Axelrod

■ Technical Data

Gross Square Feet:
1,230

Location:
Winston-Salem,
North Carolina

Type:
Wood frame

Materials:
Wood framing, vinyl siding, concrete slab, batt insulation, vinyl windows, aluminum standing-seam roof, vinyl tile, ceramic tile, gypsum wallboard

Estimated Cost to Build:
$60,000

Estimated Cost to Heat/Cool:
N/A

Locust Avenue

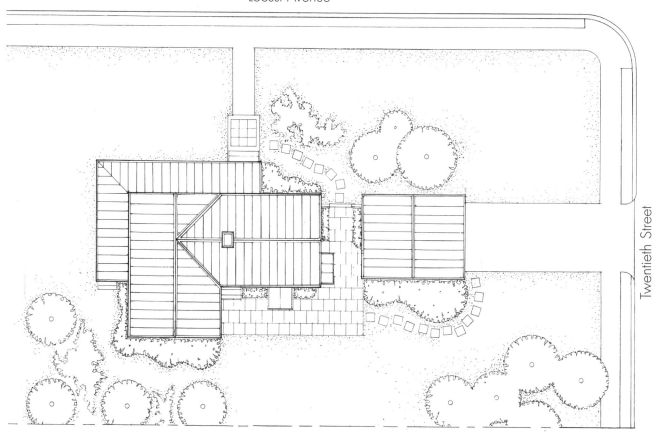

Twentieth Street

Site Plan

Floor Plans

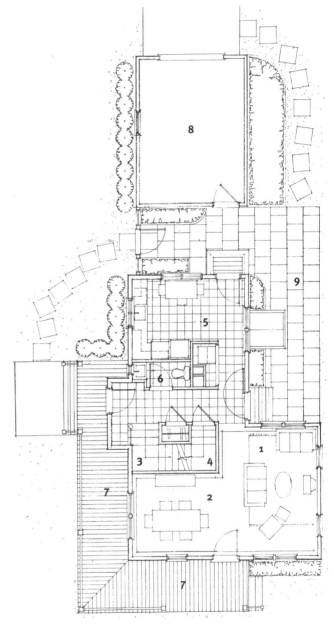

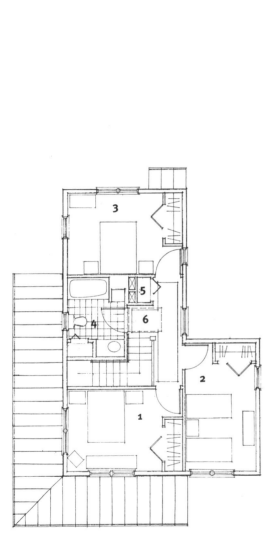

Second Floor

1 Master Bedroom
2 Bedroom 1
3 Bedroom 2 or Office
4 Bathroom
5 Linen Closet
6 Hallway

First Floor

1 Living Room
2 Dining Room
3 Stair to 2nd Floor
4 Stair to Basement
5 Kitchen
6 Bathroom
7 Covered Porch
8 Garage
9 Outdoor Terrace at Rear Yard

Elevations

West   South

North   East

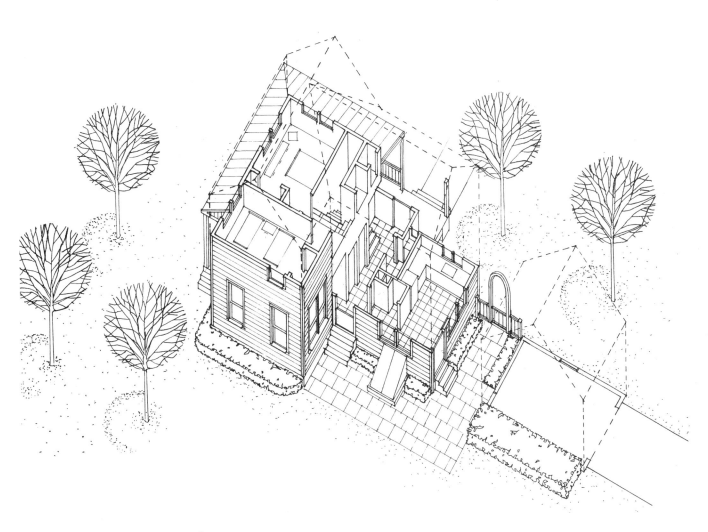

Axonometric

Perspective

BLAKE

This home combines practical and eclectic elements from an American past. The designer refers to his philosophy and concept as romantic modernism. The idea of a cottage in the forest naturally works rather nicely, given an open, functional interior.

My approach to design is the pursuit of a romantic modernism: the rigorous confluence of both efficiency and charm. All too many small contemporary houses emphasize one at the expense of the other. Conscientious design can revel in both, and does so without being expensive.

The cottage nestled deep in the woods recalls childhood fairy tales. This winter residence alludes to these images through the use of the steeply pitched roof, the wrap-around porch, and the projected bays. The walls dematerialize in the main living space, allowing residents to feel as if they are sitting under a light canopy in the midst of the forest. The layering of the columns provides a constructed forest, as a foreground to the natural one beyond.

The zoning of spaces in the house is considered in both plan and section. In plan, the division is between private and public: the resident arrives from within the cover of the garage, whereas visitors ascend the exterior stairs to the foyer, which brings them to the extended room. In section, the division emphasizes occupancy and environmental control: when only the first floor is occupied, the second floor can be completely closed off to reduce the amount of energy required to heat the inhabited space. Employing the most efficient principles of mechanical systems, bathroom plumbing is stacked, the heating system is forced air, and the main duct runs in a plenum under the stairs to service each floor.

Christopher Blake

Gross Square Feet:
1,250

Location:
Snowy regions of the United States

Type:
Wood frame

Materials:
Wood, aluminum siding and windows, standing-seam metal roof

Estimated Cost to Build:
$125,000

Estimated Cost to Heat/Cool:
N/A

Site Plan

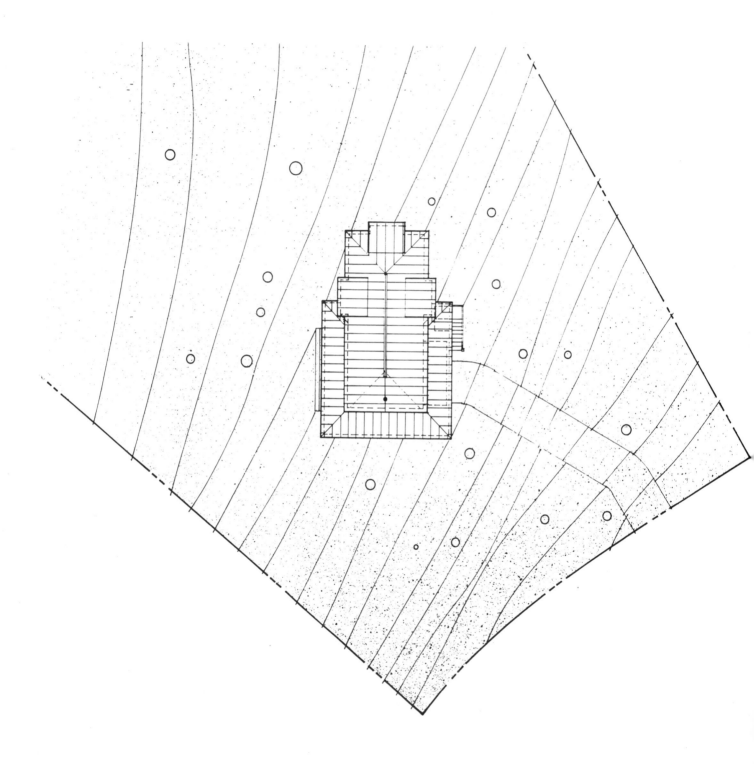

Floor Plans

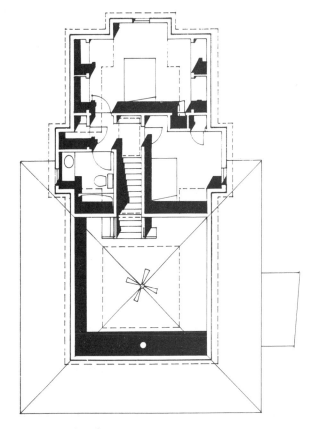

Second Floor

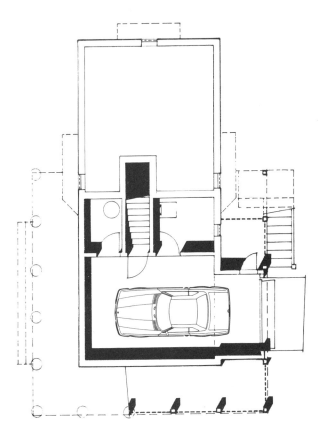

Basement

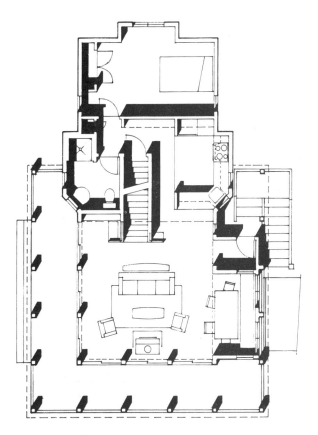

First Floor

Elevations

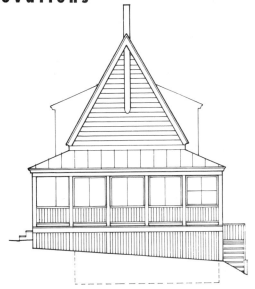

South

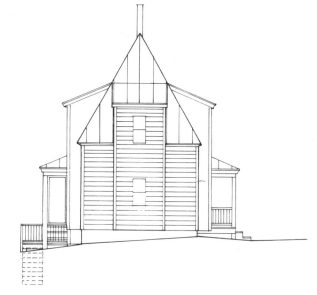

North

East

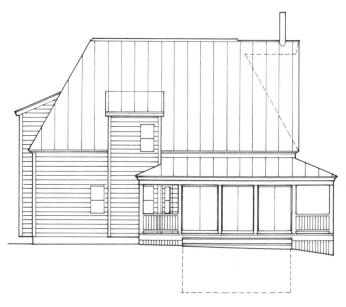

West

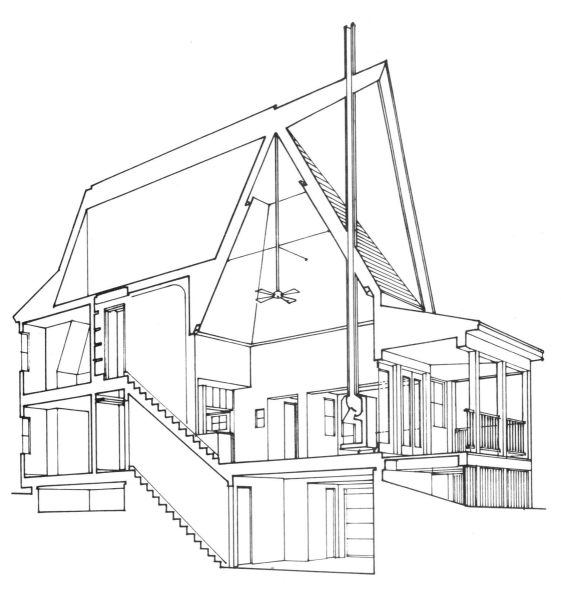

Section

Perspective

BOEHM

A multilevel, multifunctional home that could be modified in numerous ways to accommodate the occupant. A strong interior-exterior relationship exists, and the carport is integrated with the house. Windows have been placed to provide privacy and light.

The rectangular configuration and mostly blind side wall (west) allow for siting on small lots (rural, suburban, or urban) while still maintaining privacy. The primary living space is barnlike (20 feet high), with a loft over the back portion, giving occupants both light and openness plus protection and shelter. The space can be occupied in many different ways, depending upon the season and the lifestyle of the occupants. The stairs perform a number of roles: bringing high, filtered light into the entry; acting as the hallway to the bathroom, separating it from both the private and public areas; and providing a pantry/washroom at the half-level below, near the kitchen.

Strategically placed, the windows provide privacy (at tops of walls), cross-ventilate interior spaces, warm the house in the winter, and frame the view. Broad overhangs and trellises protect the windows against the hot summer sun. The chimney serves three thermal functions: exhausting the pellet stove, venting or recirculating warm air with a two-way fan, and housing the vertical duct from the gas-fired backup furnace.

The integration of lightweight, insulating masonry block at the base roots the building into the landscape and lends a quality of permanence not typically found in stick construction. Exterior spaces form habitable thresholds, buffering the interior from the elements while gaining the protection of walls and overhangs. Although integrated with the house as a part of the entry sequence, the carport could eventually be used as a studio/workspace or converted into an additional bedroom.

William H. Boehm

Gross Square Feet:
995

Location:
Mascoma Lake, New Hampshire

Type:
Wood frame

Materials:
Aerated concrete block, 2 x 6 frame, cellulose insulation, "katawba" hardboard siding, OSB lumber (recycled wood pulp), aluminum windows, standing-seam metal roofing

Estimated Cost to Build:
$110,000

Estimated Cost to Heat/Cool:
$500 per year

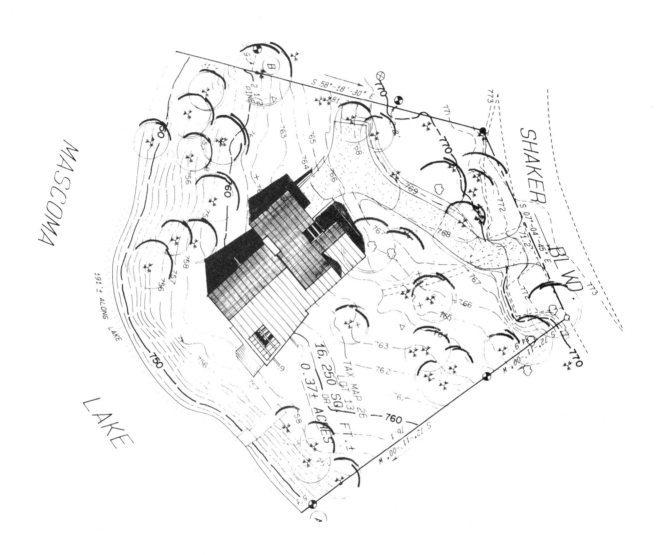

Site Plan

Floor Plans

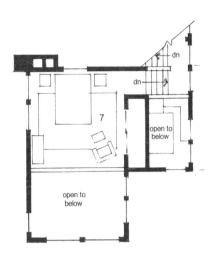

Loft

Main Level

1 Carport
2 Entry
3 Dining
4 Kitchen
5 Living
6 Deck
7 Bedroom
8 Bathroom
9 Laundry
10 Mechanical
11 Basement

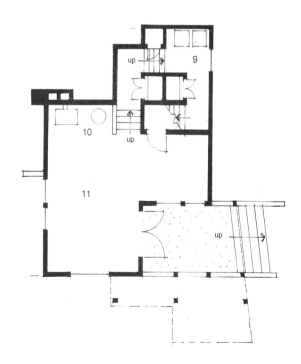

Basement

Elevations

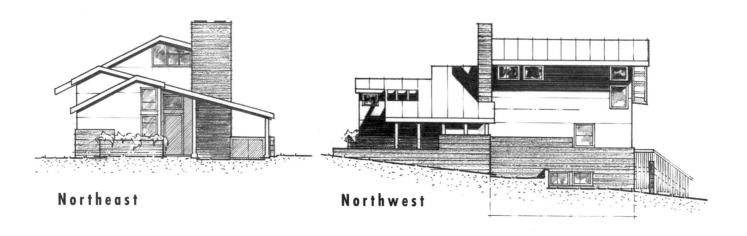

Northeast

Northwest

Southwest

Southeast

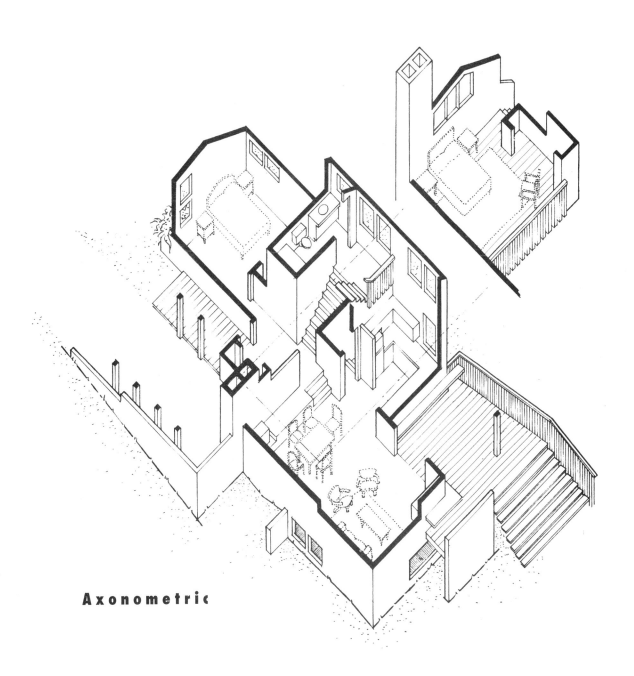

Axonometric

Perspective

CORKILL

Jury Comments

An attractive, purposeful small home that would comfortably accommodate a family. Both the exterior and interior are appealing. The rooms are spread out on a single floor but logically linked to complement these adjacencies.

The design concept for this home evolved after seeing a lakeside property, secluded and surrounded by rolling hills covered with tall evergreen trees, in Wisconsin. My idea is to provide a home or summer place that would blend with the existing environment.

A small entryway expands into a large open interior space. The home features a very open kitchen, dining room, and family room. Vaulted ceilings in the main area provide inhabitants a feeling of greater space. The family room opens onto a deck area that overlooks the lake to the north. Windows on the south side have been limited to reduce solar heating of the interior.

The eight major vertical elements that appear to subdivide the home from east to west support the ridge beams for the roof structure. These elements correspond to the rolling hills around the site. A standing-seam metal roof will reduce maintenance costs, while its forest-green color will complement the surrounding foliage.

A geothermal water pump provides heating and cooling as well as hot water. All rooms have ceiling fans and operable windows that allow for natural cooling at night. All appliances and fixtures are water efficient.

James M. Corkill

Technical Data

Gross Square Feet:
1,200

Location:
Wisconsin Dells, Wisconsin

Type:
Wood frame on concrete block foundation

Materials:
Concrete block foundation, wood frame construction faced with stucco, standing-seam metal roof, vinyl flooring, carpet

Estimated Cost to Build:
$96,000

Estimated Cost to Heat/Cool:
$1,200 per year

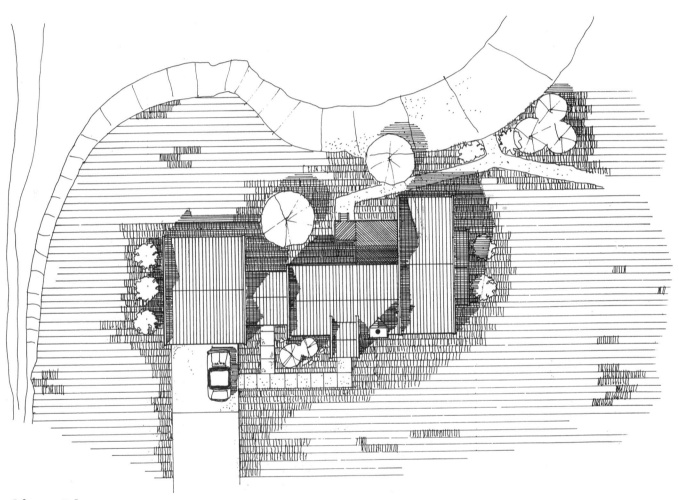

Site Plan

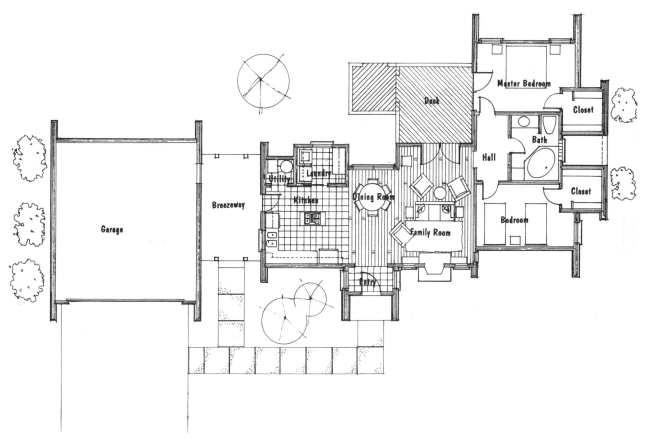

Floor Plan

Elevations

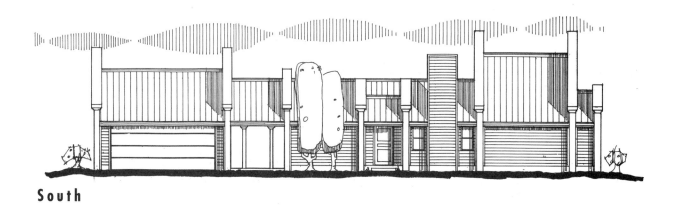

South

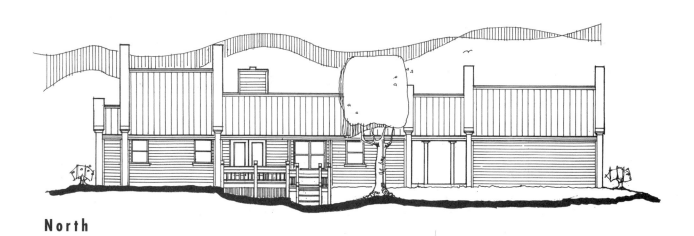

North

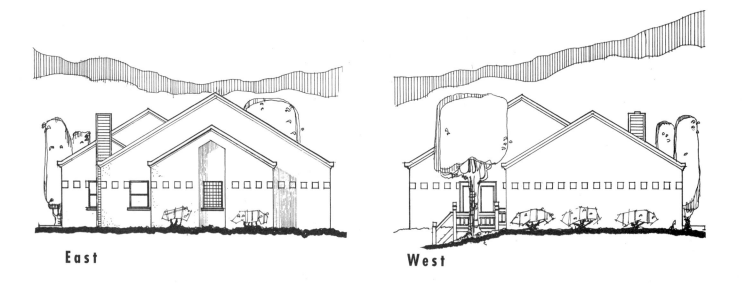

East

West

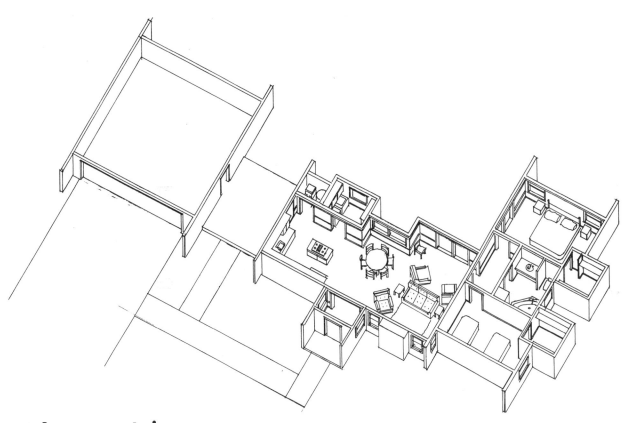

Axonometric

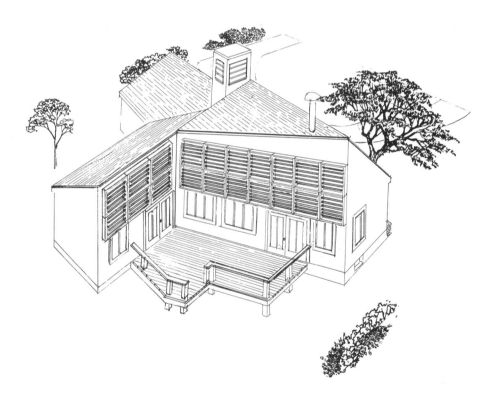

Perspective

FINIGAN

The well-conceived interior spaces of this home should prove very functional. The house has an excellent solar system and can fit into conventional neighborhoods. There is a clear influence from rural public-assembly structures and from the works of Frank Lloyd Wright.

The "Solar Ranch" brings relatively unobtrusive, high-performance, active solar heating and passive cooling to conventional suburban neighborhoods in an elevation-flexible, fundamental box. The design arises from an arrangement and rescaling of five 10-foot by 20-foot function-labeled modules. The resulting fundamental envelope configuration allows flexible solar positioning and a variety of floor plans and elevations.

Primary solar features include a Mylar "Space Blanket" vapor barrier (80 percent thermally reflective), a cooling tower, and a semiautomatic, active, liquid-convection solar heating system intended for areas with 4,000 to 8,000 heating degree days. This system is capable of building up a charge in excess of 10 million Btus.

Ten 320-square-foot wall-mounted collector boxes, containing approximately 2,000 feet of 1-inch low-emissivity/high-absorption coated copper tubing, are covered with single-pane low-E glass and use antifreeze as the medium. Heat storage employs a pressurized, insulated, 2,500-gallon coated concrete storage tank, installed vertically in the cellar below floor grade. Where a cellar is not feasible, a coated steel tank may be located horizontally in the garage.

Other solar heating components include (1) the delivery system: two-zone, thermostatically controlled, radiant floor coils, with a back-up electric furnace and temperature-activated storage tank bypass; (2) the collector night shield: storage-tank-to-storage-tank collector bypass and one-way directional valves; and (3) domestic hot water heating: preheating of the cold water supply via a coil looped through a thermal storage tank, with a back-up electric water heater.

James F. Finigan

Gross Square Feet:
1,000

Location:
Northeast United States

Type:
Wood frame

Materials:
Concrete, wood framing, Mylar "Space Blanket" vapor barrier, lightweight concrete over crushed stone

Estimated Cost to Build:
$80,000

Estimated Cost to Heat/Cool:
Up to $200 per year

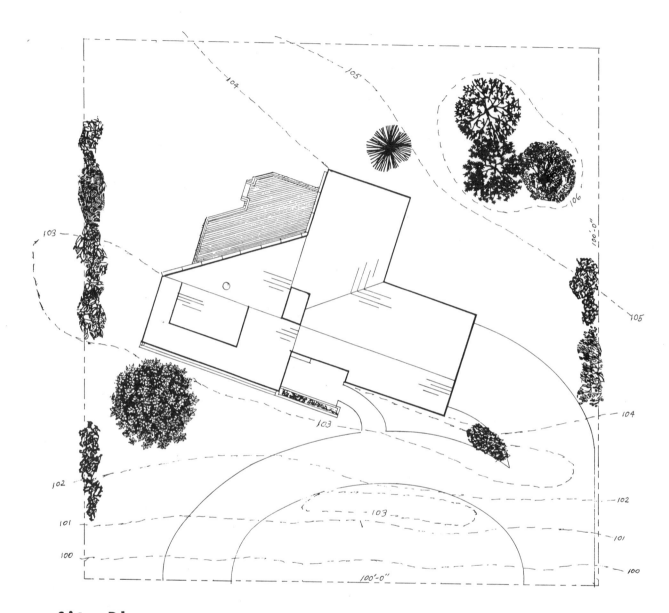

Site Plan

Floor Plans

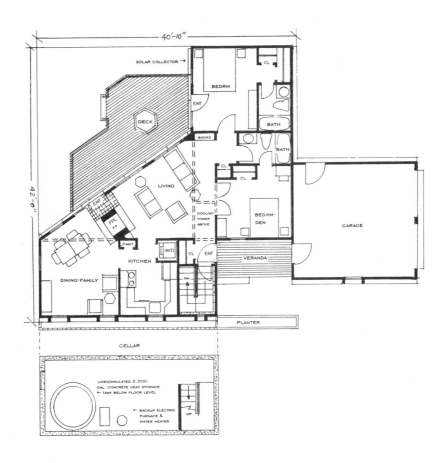

SOLAR COLLECTOR →

BEDRM

CL

ENT

BATH

BATH

DECK

BOOKS

CL

CL

LIVING

COOLING TOWER ABOVE

ENT

FPL

BEDRM-DEN

GARAGE

PANT.

W/D

CL ENT

VERANDA

KITCHEN

DN

DINING-FAMILY

PLANTER

40'-10"

42'-0"

CELLAR

LINED/INSULATED 2,500 GAL CONCRETE HEAT STORAGE
← TANK BELOW FLOOR LEVEL

← BACKUP ELECTRIC FURNACE & WATER HEATER

UP

Alternate

53

Elevations

Southeast

Northeast

Southwest

Northwest

Axonometric

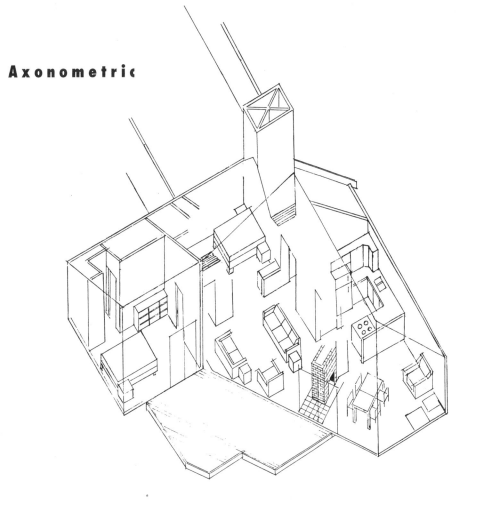

Schematic: Active Solar Heating System

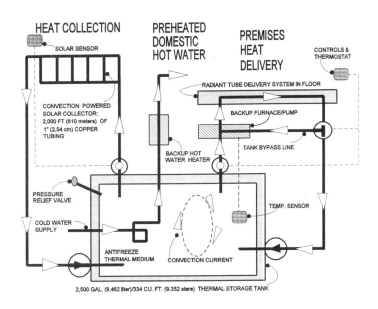

HEAT COLLECTION

SOLAR SENSOR

CONVECTION POWERED
SOLAR COLLECTOR:
2,000 FT (610 meters) OF
1" (2.54 cm) COPPER
TUBING

PRESSURE
RELIEF VALVE

COLD WATER
SUPPLY

ANTIFREEZE
THERMAL MEDIUM

CONVECTION CURRENT

2,500 GAL. (9,462 liter)/334 CU. FT. (9.352 stere) THERMAL STORAGE TANK

**PREHEATED
DOMESTIC
HOT WATER**

BACKUP HOT
WATER HEATER

**PREMISES
HEAT
DELIVERY**

CONTROLS &
THERMOSTAT

RADIANT TUBE DELIVERY SYSTEM IN FLOOR

BACKUP FURNACE/PUMP

TANK BYPASS LINE

TEMP. SENSOR

NOTES

1. Minimum thermostat
tank shutoff temperature
is 80°F.

2. Collector tubing coated
with low-E, high absorp-
tion materials

3. Vertical angle of
collector boxes will
vary depending upon
latitudes

NO SCALE

SYMBOL KEY

 ONE WAY CHECK VALVE

 ONE-WAY SHUTOFF CONTROL VALVE

 DIRECTIONAL CONTROL VALVE

Perspective

FLEMING

A traditional design that would appeal to many homeowners. Simple, compact, and efficient, this house would fit into almost any neighborhood. There is a nice interior-exterior relationship in this design.

This is a Midwestern home in every sense, abstractly based on simple farmhouse plans of earlier times. The house is compact and efficient. Outdoor spaces are modest in size but integral to the overall scheme. The sloping site allows the basement level to provide additional living space, as a walk-out.

The primary design focus is a two-story volume, around which the remainder of the plan is organized. From an interior standpoint this creates a sense of spaciousness. From a practical standpoint it provides excellent natural ventilation with the use of an attic fan. The interior balcony also serves a dual role. It allows for spatial communication between the master bedroom and the living room, enhancing the natural ventilation, but also provides a needed sense of scale to the upper portion of the

two-story space — scale that is conspicuously absent from most vaulted rooms in homes today.

The exterior spaces complement the interior spaces and feature a screened porch off the dining room. The dining room also offers access to a generous deck, from which stairs descend to a patio at the walk-out level.

The siting of the house provides an island of tended lawn and plantings within a more natural setting. A pergola connects the house with a two-car garage that buffers the house from northerly winter winds. Other small structures rim the tended lawn.

Jeffrey Fleming

■ Technical Data

Gross Square Feet:
1,237

Location:
Midwestern United States site in a semi-rural or rural context

Type:
Wood frame

Materials:
Concrete block foundation; wood frame walls; cedar siding, trim, and deck; fieldstone; prefinished aluminum windows; hardwood flooring; ceramic tile; carpet

Estimated Cost to Build:
$117,000

Estimated Cost to Heat/Cool:
$300–$400 per year

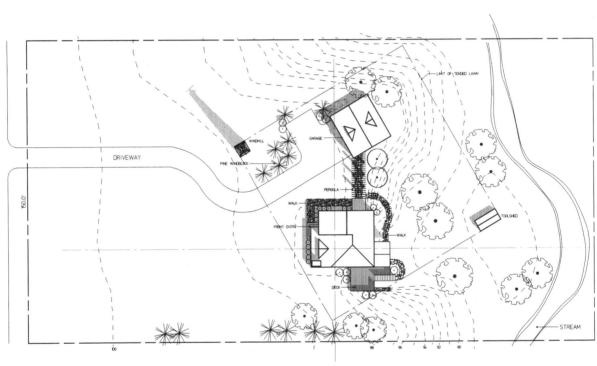

DRIVEWAY

150.0'

WINDMILL

PINE WINDBLOCK

GARAGE

LIMIT OF TENDED LAWN

PERGOLA

WALK

FRONT ENTRY

WALK

TOOLSHED

DECK

STREAM

100   98   96   94   92   90

Site Plan

Floor Plans

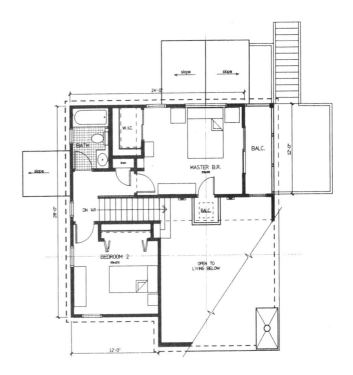

Second Level

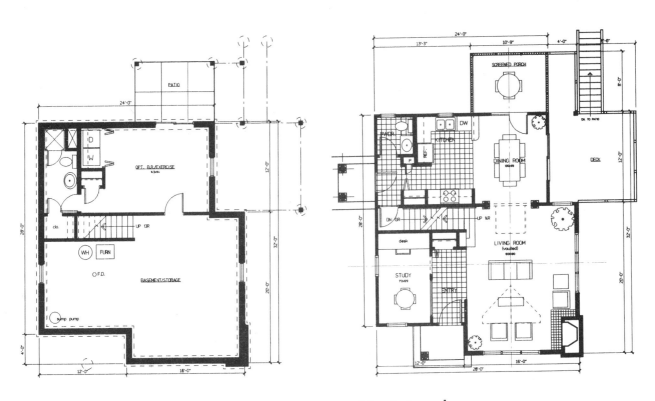

Foundation/Basement

First Level

Elevations

North

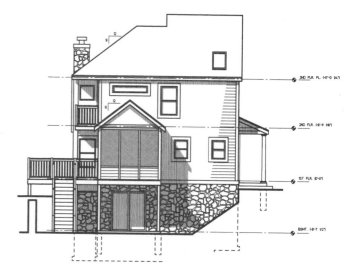

East

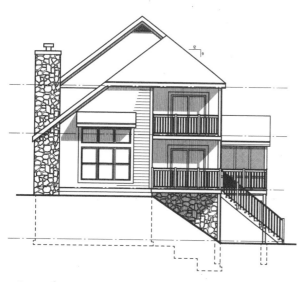

South

West

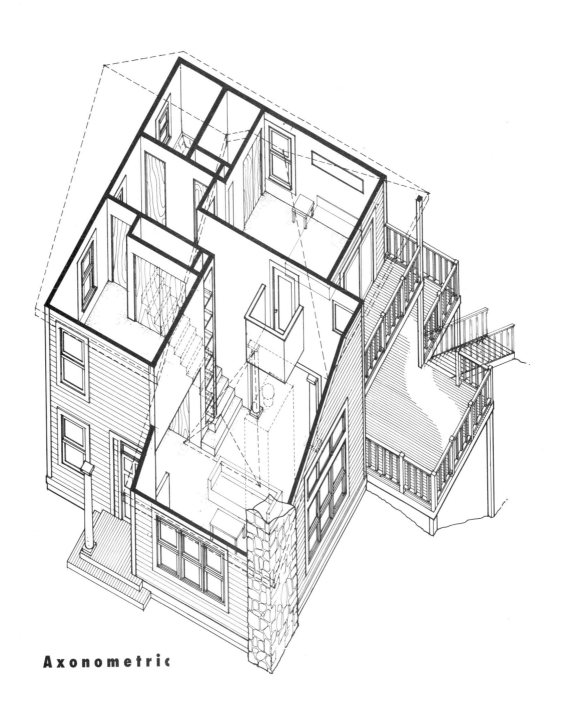

Axonometric

Perspective

KING

■ Jury Comments

An attractive, open interior plan accommodating flexible traffic patterns. The decking on three sides adds to both the aesthetic and functional characteristics of the home. The environmentally conscious design fits in nicely with the landscape.

Designed for a professional couple, this compact single-family house occupies a level, circular lot in Pinecrest, near Whistler, British Columbia. The two-story design reflects the owners' desire for informal comfort, privacy, views, and a rusticity that blends with the natural environment. Siting was influenced by the circular lot, a nearby marshy pond, and adjoining developments, as well as by the owners' wish to preserve as many of the adjacent trees as possible.

Approached from the southwest, the building is oriented towards the sun and the views. A raised wooden deck wraps around the base of the house; a wide overhang on the south side protects it from sun and wind. Reached via a covered stairway, the functionally compact entry expands immediately into a large two-and-a-half-story living space illuminated by a large east-facing window. The window adds visual dimension and view space as well as a feeling of integration with the forest.

Smaller dining and kitchen areas with adjacent service/storage space complete the simple, rectangular ground-floor plan. Accessible by stairway, a second-story bedroom wing and hallway overlook the informal living space, where an overhead fan aids air circulation.

Environmentally appropriate and naturally beautiful, wood constitutes the major structural and finishing component; it offers economy, aesthetics, low maintenance, flexibility, and compatibility. Energy-conservation features include a Naxcor insulation system, tightly sealed junctions, and weather sealing with air-recovery ventilating systems.

Kenneth E. King

■ Technical Data

Gross Square Feet:
1,250 (modifications to 1,500)

Location:
Near Whistler, British Columbia, Canada (ski resort area with heavy snowfall)

Type:
Wood frame

Materials:
Metal sheet roofing, aluminum windows, gypsum wallboard, carpet, Naxcor insulation

Estimated Cost to Build:
$100,000

Estimated Cost to Heat/Cool:
N/A

Site Plan

Pinecrest

road

adjoining development

adjoining development

Site Influence Plan

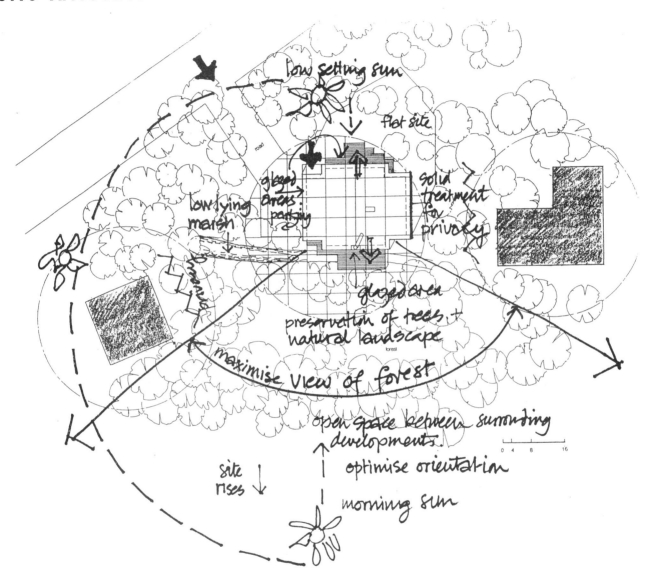

low setting sun

flat site

low lying marsh

glazed areas part22y

solid treatment for privacy

glazed area

preservation of trees + natural landscape

maximise view of forest

open space between surrounding developments.

site rises ↓

optimise orientation

morning sun

0 4 8 16

Floor Plans

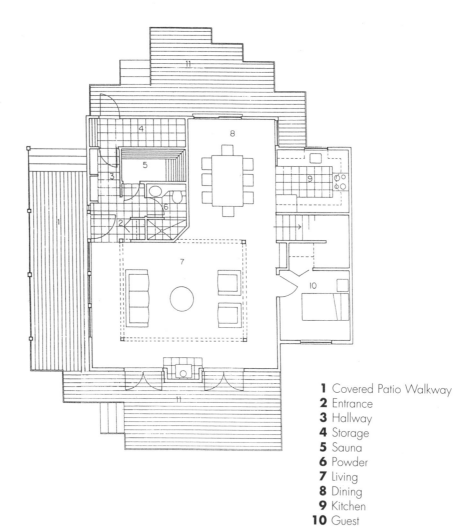

Ground Floor

1 Covered Patio Walkway
2 Entrance
3 Hallway
4 Storage
5 Sauna
6 Powder
7 Living
8 Dining
9 Kitchen
10 Guest
11 Deck

Second Floor

1 Deck
2 Master Bedroom
3 Bathroom
4 Bedroom
5 Upper Volume of Living Room

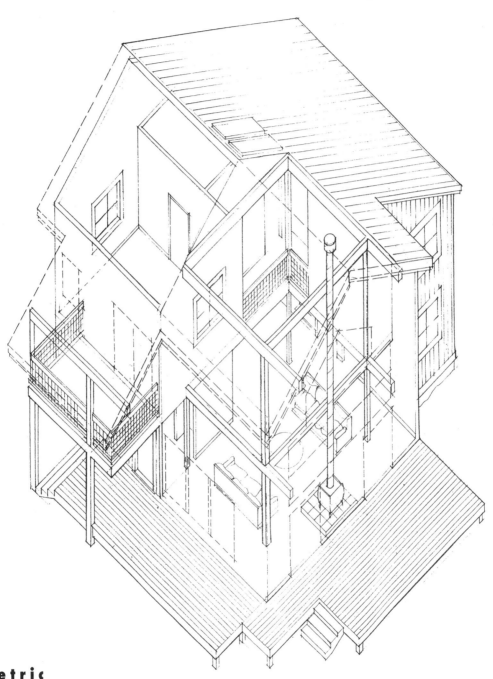

Axonometric

Perspective

TSANG

A small house that successfully conveys the illusion of greater space. Ideal for a long, narrow lot, the design incorporates energy-efficient features.

The objective of this house design was to achieve the most with the least: it uses simplicity, flexibility, and economy to achieve an organic, ecological, and environmental synthesis. Located in southern Ontario and economical to construct, the house efficiently uses both space and energy. To provide richness in spatial expression and experience, the design lets the inhabitants wake up to, and perform most major activities with, the sun. Window seats, covered porch, open balconies, and decks offer variety.

The greenhouse/patio provides for indoor gardening and outdoor living space. With its 8-foot ceiling, the basement may be turned into a den/office or a bedroom

(especially desirable if raised) or a walkout basement. Landscaping on site promotes a variety of outdoor activities and experiences.

The design realizes energy savings through the southern orientation, the landscaping, the use of environmentally friendly and recyclable materials, and energy-efficient systems. Materials and components, including a combination natural gas furnace and heat-recovery ventilator, were chosen to achieve the lowest energy impact and costs. Energy-saving plumbing and electric fixtures further reduce waste. Thus the house is designed to reduce, reuse, and recycle.

Remus S. L. Tsang

Technical Data

Gross Square Feet:
1,025

Location:
Northern climate, southern Ontario, Canada

Type:
Wood stud wall construction, precast concrete foundation walls, factory-built roof trusses

Materials:
Steel roofing, pressed scrap wood siding, drywall (25 percent recycled wastes), hardwood flooring, tile (recycled glass), carpet (recycled plastic), double-glazed windows filled with argon gas

Estimated Cost to Build:
$65,000

Estimated Cost to Heat/Cool:
$120 for heating and $70 for cooling per year

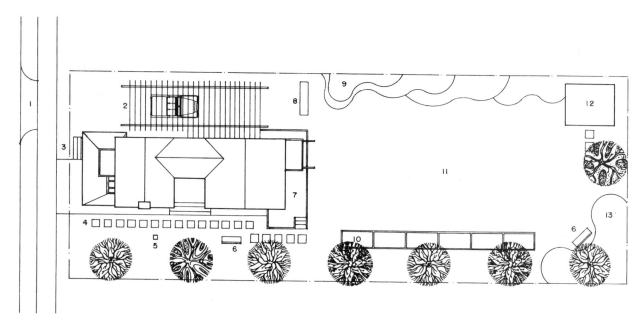

Site Plan

1 Driveway
2 Carport
3 Entry
4 Walkway
5 Sculpture
6 Bench
7 Deck
8 Storage
9 Rock Formation/Garden
10 Trellis Walk
11 Play Area
12 Hot Tub/Sauna
13 Landscaped Area

Floor Plans

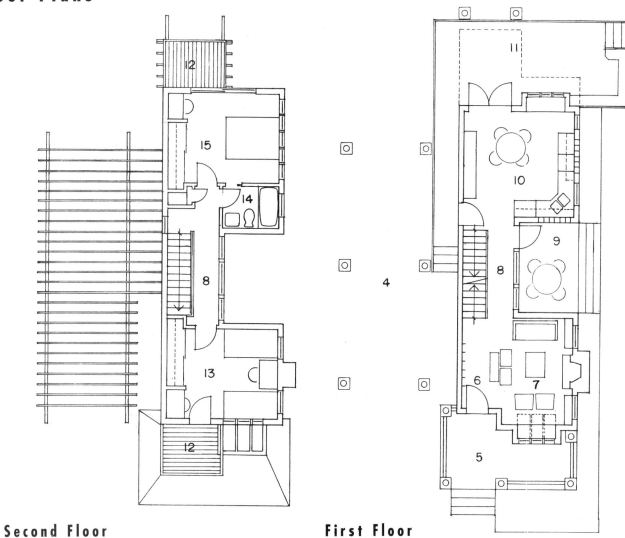

Second Floor

First Floor

1 Future Washroom
2 Furnace
3 Recreation
4 Carport
5 Porch
6 Entry
7 Living
8 Passage
9 Greenhouse/Patio
10 Kitchen/Dining
11 Deck
12 Balcony
13 Bedroom
14 Washroom
15 Master Bedroom

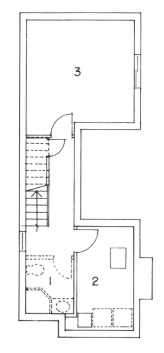

Basement

Elevations

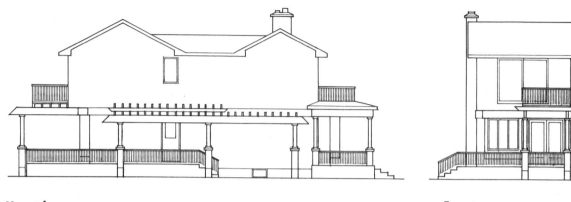

North

East

South

West

Axonometrics

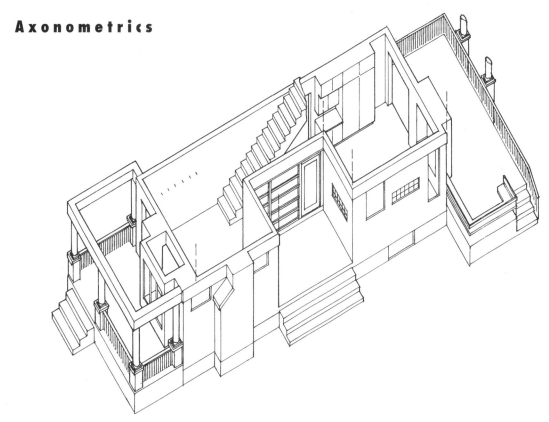

First Level

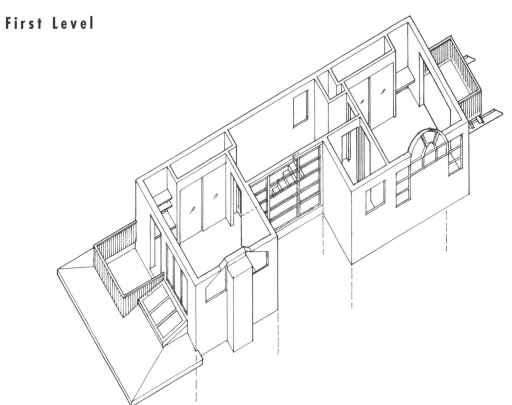

Second Level

Perspective

VERHIEL

Here, an attempt has been made to focus each room towards a different view. The illusion of a larger home is accomplished by incorporating a deck and wooden fence and by separating the garage from the house. The energy-efficient design takes advantage of the sun's radiant heating in the winter.

This small house is a metaphoric "ark" that has settled on a cliff edge. Built on a wooden deck (raft), its clapboard/wood-panel walls contain a free-flowing open plan for the public space. A spiral staircase leads to the private rooms, which push up through the roof form, almost like a ship's bridge. The walls, with carefully placed openings, allow cross-axial views through the living space and to the four cardinal views and vistas. This superimposes the activities of domestic living onto the natural environment, and vice versa.

One enters the site through a pergola that accommodates vines and flowers. From this semi-interior space that leads through the forest and meadow, one steps onto the edge of the deck and enters the deep porch. This gradual transition between exterior and interior attempts to blur the distinction between the two.

The entryway, articulated as a glazed box with built-in window seat, reveals the four main views in varying degrees. Bay windows help to extend the spaces into the landscape. Built-in furniture pieces guide activities within the structure.

Clerestory windows provide ambient light as well as induce air convection. The fireplace and stack stand central in the plan and, with appropriate venting and the aid of a natural gas furnace, heat the entire house. The south wall with its large over-hang not only frames the site's best view, but also exposes the house to natural breezes and the sun's radiant heating in winter months.

Andy Verhiel

Technical Data

Gross Square Feet:
1,150

Location:
North Shore, Vancouver, British Columbia, Canada

Type:
Large wood member and stud frame construction on concrete pier

Materials:
Wood, slightly sloped copper roofing, wood casement windows, clapboard/wood-panel walls

Estimated Cost to Build:
$160,000

Estimated Cost to Heat/Cool:
$1,000 per year

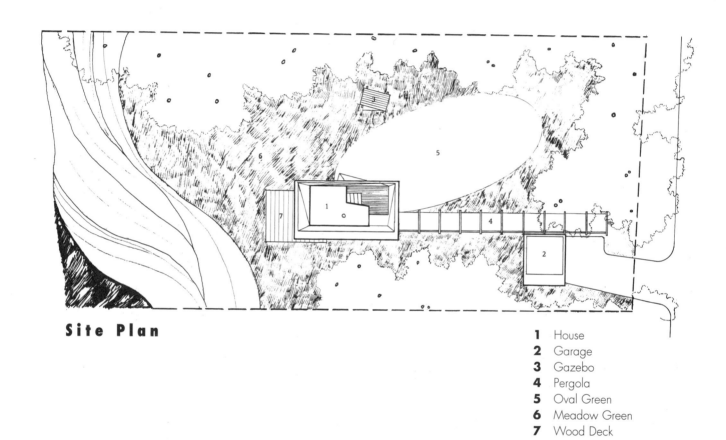

Site Plan

1 House
2 Garage
3 Gazebo
4 Pergola
5 Oval Green
6 Meadow Green
7 Wood Deck

Floor Plans

1 Entry
2 Living Room
3 Reading Alcove
4 Dining Room
5 Kitchen
6 Laundry/Storage
7 Bathroom
8 Bedroom

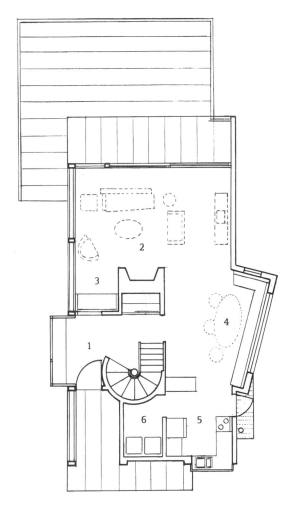

First Floor

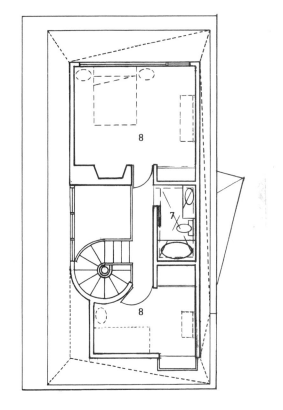

Second Floor

Elevations

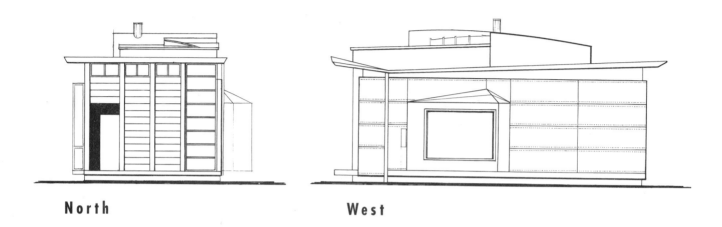

North

West

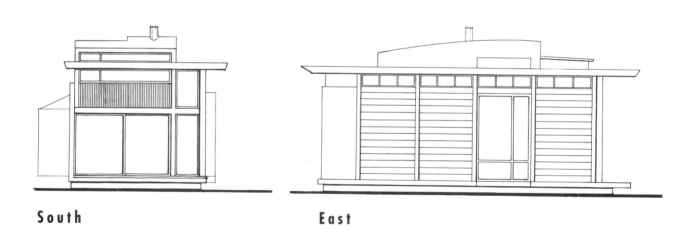

South

East

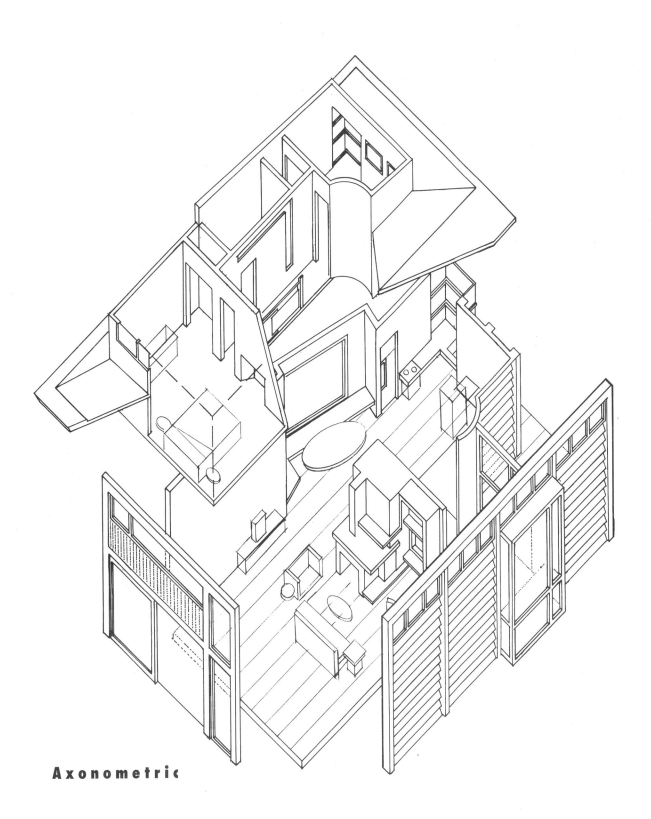

Axonometric

Model

WAGNER

An open, sensible plan with plenty of windows for natural light. Depending on the site, the exterior appearance could be very good. All elements combine to give this home a functional look.

This small house sits at the top of a ridge overlooking the panoramic views of Vermont's beautiful landscape.

Approaching the site from the west, one travels on a winding driveway that wraps around a manmade pond. Passing to the main level of the house, the viewer finds the rear facade celebrating the valley below with floor-to-ceiling windows. Only a few partitions define the different spaces, making the interior aesthetic of the house rustic and lofty. By using such materials such as wood, masonry, and granite, the interior captures the warmth of its natural surroundings.

The house features a shift of two equal parts from east to west, linked by the overlapping space that they share. This break implies two parts to the whole, with the common link then forming the place of assembly throughout the floor plan. At any place in the house, one can always refer back to the common meeting place. On the first floor, no divisions separate the viewer from the place of assembly. Even outside, one can maintain a visual conversation with activities in the common area. On the second floor, the use of the double-height space allows the viewer to be in constant contact with the happenings below.

Eric Wagner

Technical Data

Gross Square Feet:
720

Location:
Vermont

Type:
Wood frame

Materials:
Wood, masonry, granite

Estimated Cost to Build:
$135,000

Estimated Cost to Heat/Cool:
$1,500 per year

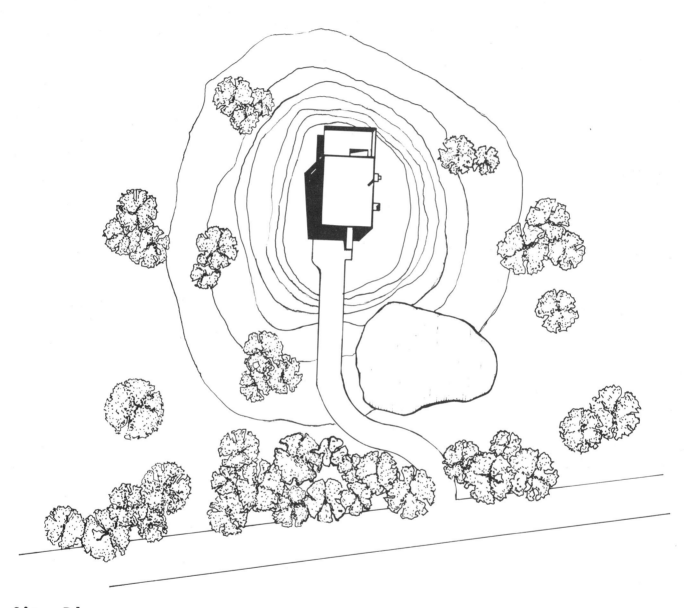

Site Plan

Floor Plans

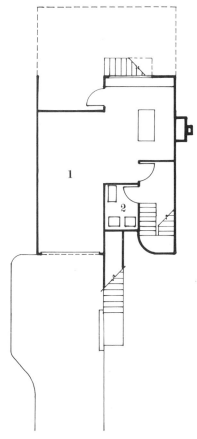

Ground Level

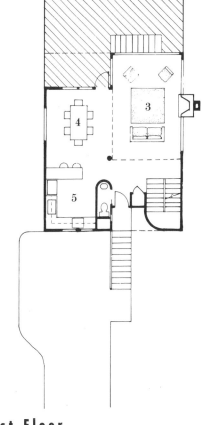

First Floor

1 Garage
2 Laundry/Mechanical
3 Living Room
4 Dining Room
5 Kitchen
6 Bedroom

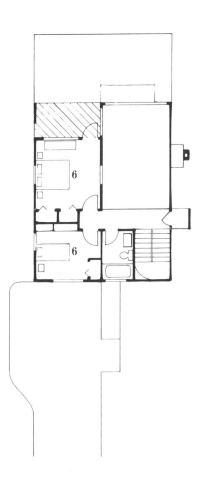

Second Floor

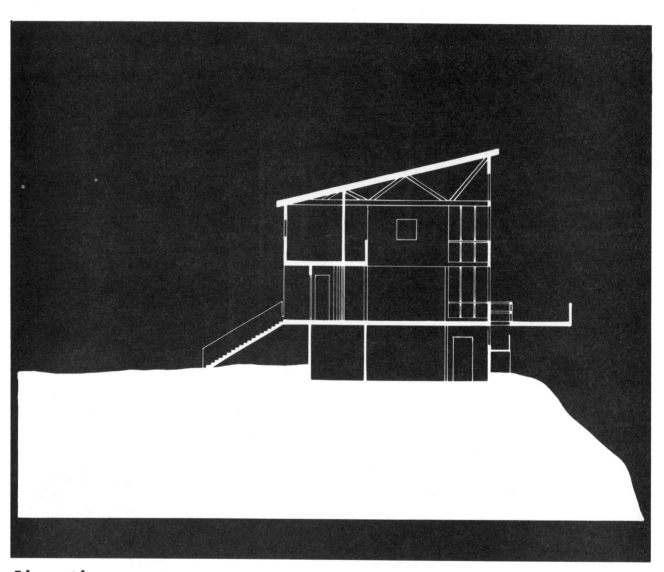

Elevation

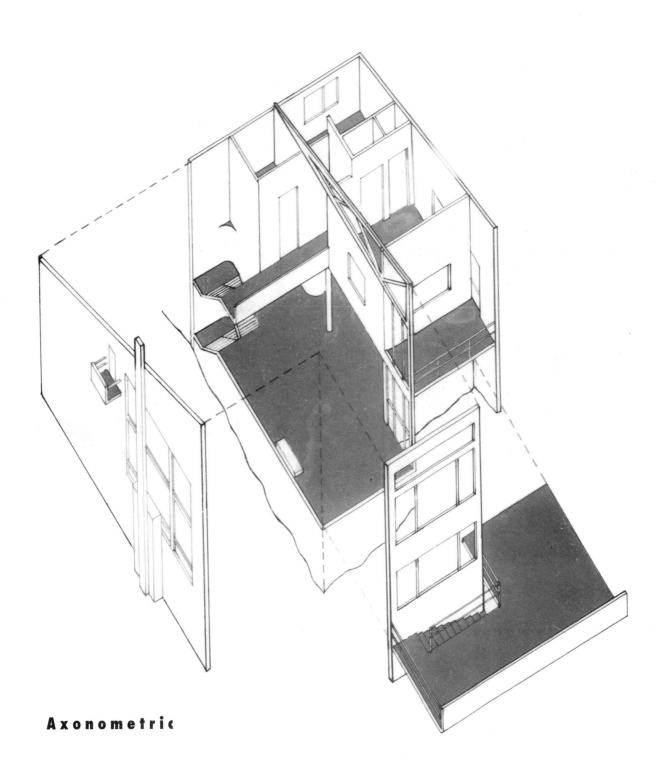

Axonometric

Perspective

LEYTHAM

■——┤Jury Comments├

A small house design that fits geographically in a multitude of settings. Inexpensive, energy efficient, and appropriate for many clients. A light-sensitive interior must consider trees for summer shade. The unique masonry stove and chimney provide a radiant heat system.

Design is the process of simplifying a problem to achieve an elegant solution. The "Cape" house form described here is simple to build and very efficient. Sculpting this simple form adapts it to the land and to the need for young professionals to have access to outdoor living areas. The design incorporates double use of spaces — both visually and physically. For example, the porch in summer is used as the carport in winter.

Energy-efficient design features include the airlock vestibule, passive solar in the central hall, and wood heat, which offers lower dependence on nonrenewable energy resources. A masonry stove with glass

doors has switchbacks built into the flues, which turn the mass of chimney into a radiant heat storage system in the central hall (backup with gas burner in firebox). An optional decorative stove or fireplace can be added to the master bedroom.

Expanded spaces include the two-story living room and the kitchen counter area with pass-through to the dining area. A stacked washer/dryer located in the second-floor bath is close to the source of laundry. The plan maximizes closet space. A basement can be added for storage.

Tom Leytham

■——┤Technical Data├

Gross Square Feet:
1,152

Location:
Vermont

Type:
Light wood frame

Materials:
Wood, concrete, cantilevered Cape truss

Estimated Cost to Build:
$86,400

Estimated Cost to Heat/Cool:
Over $200 per year

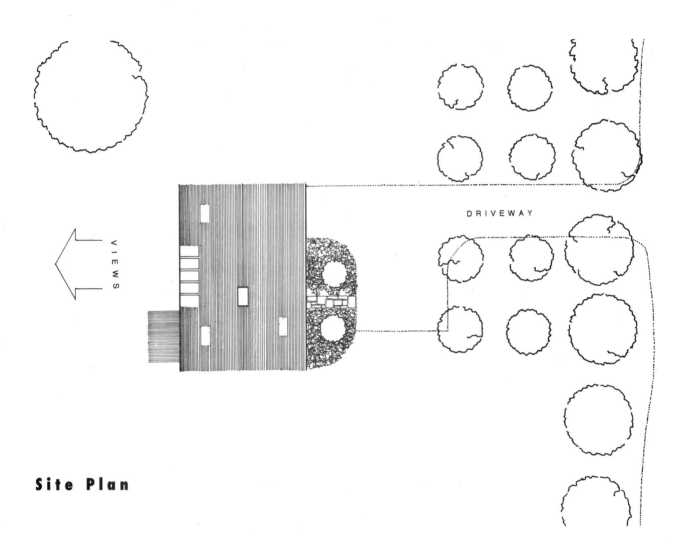

V I E W S

DRIVEWAY

Site Plan

Floor Plans

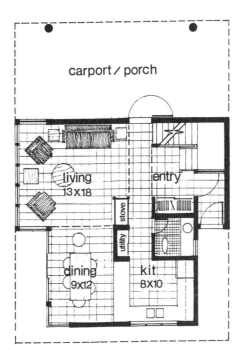

First Floor

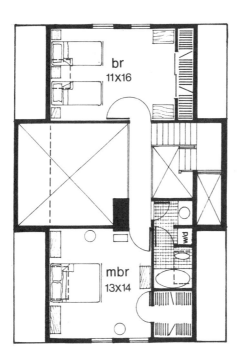

Second Floor

Elevations

South

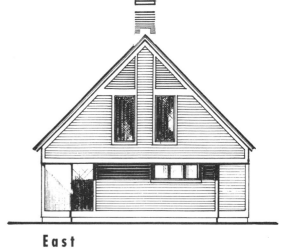

East

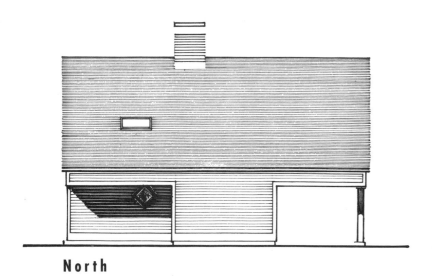

North

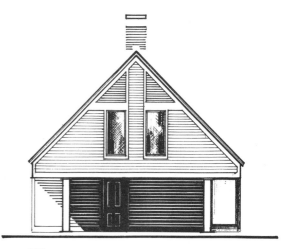

West

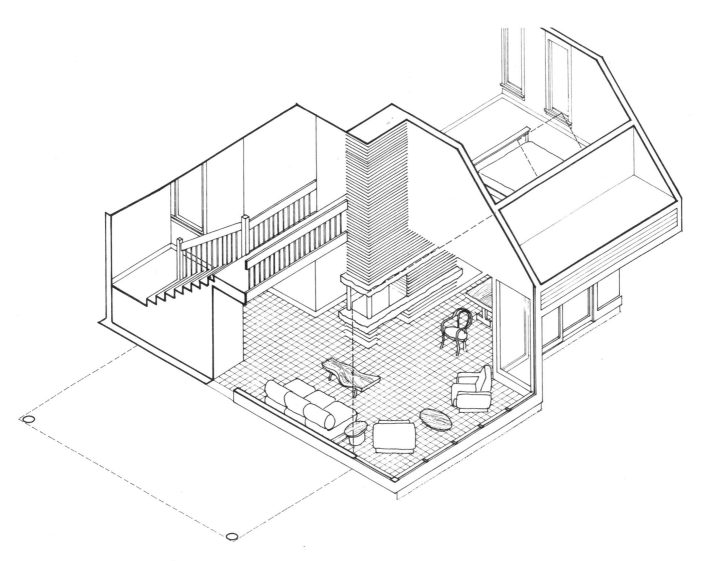

Axonometric

Perspective

MAH

░ Jury Comments

A stark reflection of the Canadian landscape with simple, clean lines. The design represents a renovated farmhouse style using contemporary materials with a rustic theme. The home has a great combination of energy-efficient and water-conserving features.

The house is designed to capture sun for both heat and light. Since the south side faces a neighboring house that will shade the lower level, a garage is placed on that side. This gesture accommodates a two-story scheme, which is set back from the neighboring property line to allow light to enter. Light from the upper level illuminates the living area via the open stairwell, with long overhangs to shade the hot summer sun. Overhangs are used extensively to mediate both light and heat.

In response to cold winters, the highly insulated and tightly sealed house has front and back porches, which act as airlock entries. In other seasons, the back exterior enclosed veranda (unheated) accommodates evening outdoor living, with operable vents and ample insect screening. During the day the veranda can be opened with overhead garage-type doors.

Active solar collectors on the roof supplement the heating of domestic hot water and the in-floor hydronic space-heating system. Zoned for the living area and sleeping area, the heating system also includes a supplementary energy-efficient gas fireplace.

A storage tank holds graywater from bathing, which pipes then convey to a storage tank that provides water for the toilet. Water collected from the roof flows either to the graywater tank or to the long masonry wall, where it is channeled to a cistern. Small amounts of rainwater from the roof are scuppered to the surrounding landscape.

Lillian Mei Ngan Mah

░ Technical Data

Gross Square Feet:
1,115

Location:
Alberta, Canada

Type:
Wood frame

Materials:
2 x 6 engineered wood, cotton batts (R-20 and R-40), concrete masonry, factory-finished wood siding, low-VOC paints and other finishing materials, low-E windows

Estimated Cost to Build:
$61,000

Estimated Cost to Heat/Cool:
50 percent less than comparable homes in area

Site and Floor Plans

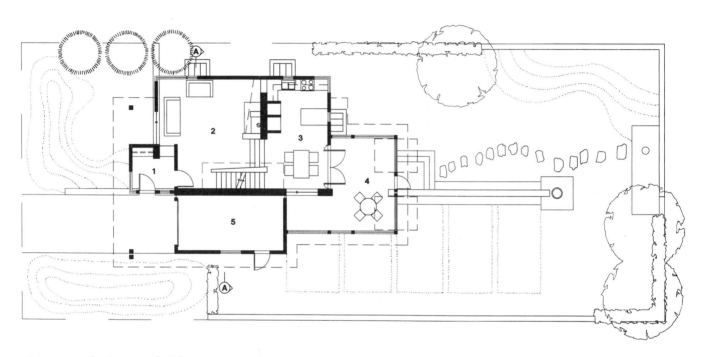

Site and Ground Floor

1 Entry Porch
2 Living Room
3 Kitchen/Dining
4 Unheated Veranda
5 Garage
6 Bedroom
7 Bathroom
8 Roof Deck
9 Basement/Laundry/Mechanical

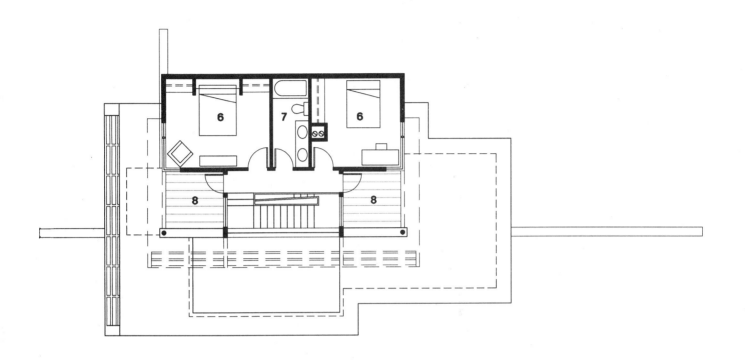

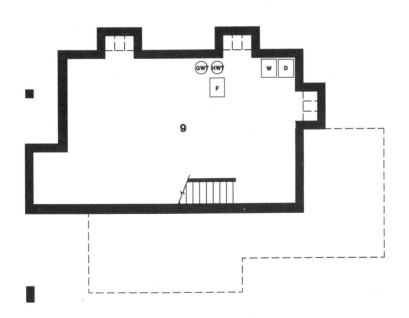

Basement

Elevations

West

East

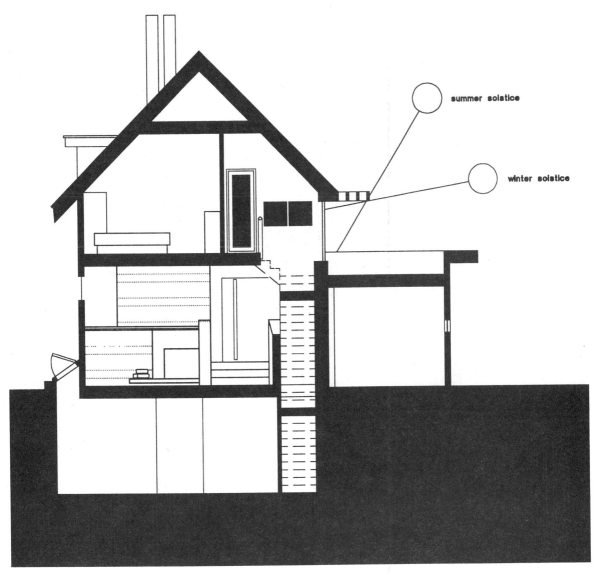

summer solstice

winter solstice

Section

Perspective

LEE & NOBLE

■ Jury Comments

This design pulls together three architectonic units — the living room and study, the kitchen and dining area, and the bedrooms — into one unified whole. The exterior of the house especially suits a rural setting.

The physical elements that go into a house, such as concrete, wood, and glass, must be combined with the spiritual ingredients that come from our collective and personal memories of the archetypal home.

This house design reflects the local West Coast vernacular architecture. The greatest inspiration for the building is the site itself. Set in a natural clearing surrounded by coniferous and deciduous trees, the house takes advantage of spectacular views of the Pacific Ocean. Located approximately twenty minutes from a downtown core, the site enjoys a forestlike setting.

The double-height element at the east end anchors the house and connects to a skylit gallery that doubles as circulation and library. The latter acts as a datum connecting sleeping, service, and living

areas. Circulation is concentrated along the north wall to serve as a buffer from the heavily used road. The living spaces open up to the south to capture the spectacular ocean views.

The Pacific Northwest climate features mild, wet winters and warm summers. Local materials — wood for framing, cedar siding, and metal roofing — are used because of their availability and durability. Cellulose insulation made of recycled newsprint is blown into the wall cavities. A natural gas furnace assisted by a wood-burning fireplace provides winter warmth. Summer cooling relies on ocean-tempered natural air currents, enhanced by the stack effect of the open loft. The trellis extending over the south terrace provides summer shading.

Eleanor Lee and Michael Noble

■ Technical Data

Gross Square Feet:
1,240

Location:
Pacific Northwest of the United States and Canada

Type:
Standard wood frame with concrete foundation

Materials:
Cedar siding, metal roof, wood windows, hardwood/tile floors, gypsum wallboard

Estimated Cost to Build:
$90,000

Estimated Cost to Heat/Cool:
$215 per year

Site Plan

Floor Plans

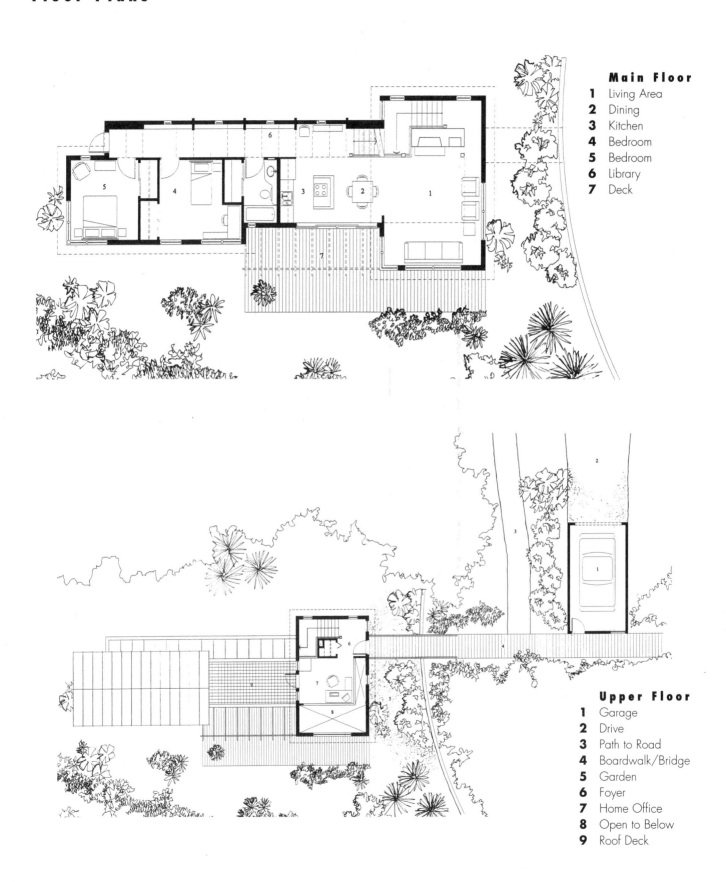

Main Floor
1 Living Area
2 Dining
3 Kitchen
4 Bedroom
5 Bedroom
6 Library
7 Deck

Upper Floor
1 Garage
2 Drive
3 Path to Road
4 Boardwalk/Bridge
5 Garden
6 Foyer
7 Home Office
8 Open to Below
9 Roof Deck

Elevations

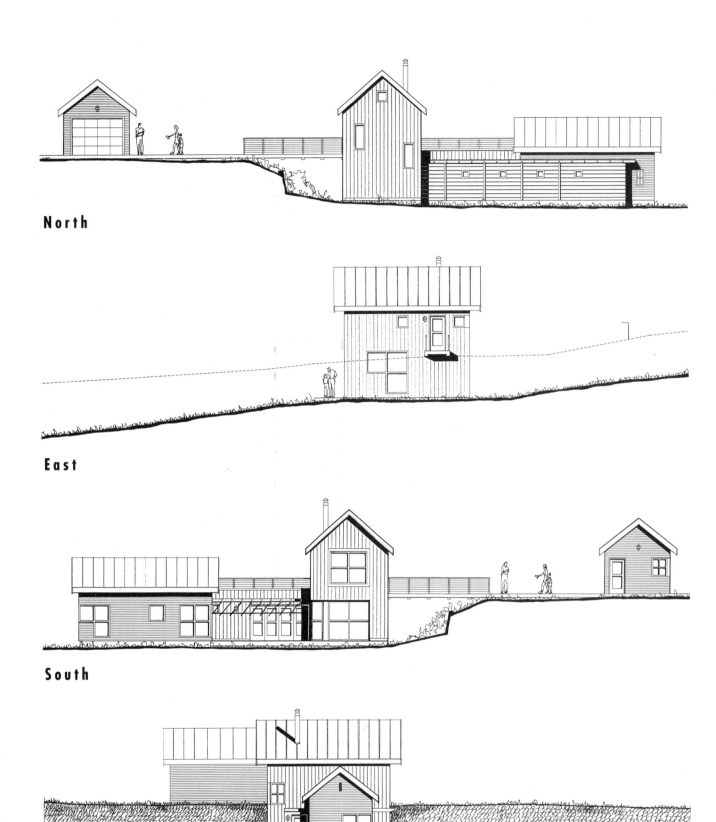

North

East

South

West

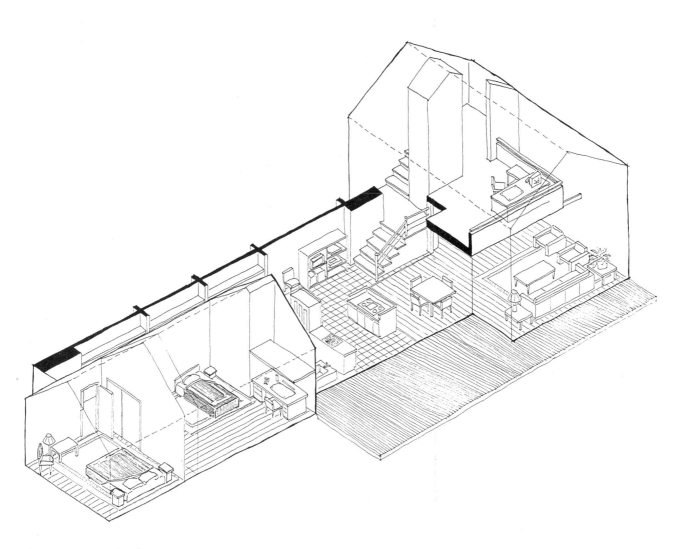

Axonometric

Perspective

OLDI CONSTRUCTIONS

Jury Comments

An economical, practical proposal that efficiently uses space. A garage might be added in certain climates. The second floor uses the A-frame concept.

Arising from nature and landscape, good architecture features simplicity and clarity, combined with environmentally friendly materials. Beauty is not just aesthetics. The old beautiful buildings were built not to meet aesthetical expectations but out of necessity, from available materials, with perfect handcraft skills.

This design is heavily influenced by cost, both to build it and to live in it. Other design considerations include size, compactness, simplicity in construction and function, durability, technological potential, and energy efficiency (for example, well-insulated floors, walls, windows, and roofs). Within these elements we look for a space that gives worthy conditions for living and a feeling of safety. We effectively use the cubic content of the house to maximize space in the day area, where family life concentrates, expanding outward to the exterior space.

The beauty emerges from the conglomerate of the logical construction, functionality, color appropriate to the environment, good materials, proper handcraft, and a little bit of something difficult to name. We want ourselves and our nearest beloved to be safe and comfortable. This is why we think about small houses for others. The kitchen, the bed, the fireplace. Wife or husband and baby playing on the warm floor. This is really enough to feel human. Small houses become beautiful in the moment when they become ours.

Olgierd Miloszewicz

Technical Data

Gross Square Feet:
1,092

Location:
Poland

Type:
Wood frame

Materials:
Concrete or stone foundation, wood frame, mineral wool, Styrofoam, vinyl siding, terra-cotta floor, drywall gypsum plaster

Estimated Cost to Build:
$50,000

Estimated Cost to Heat/Cool:
$1,300 per year

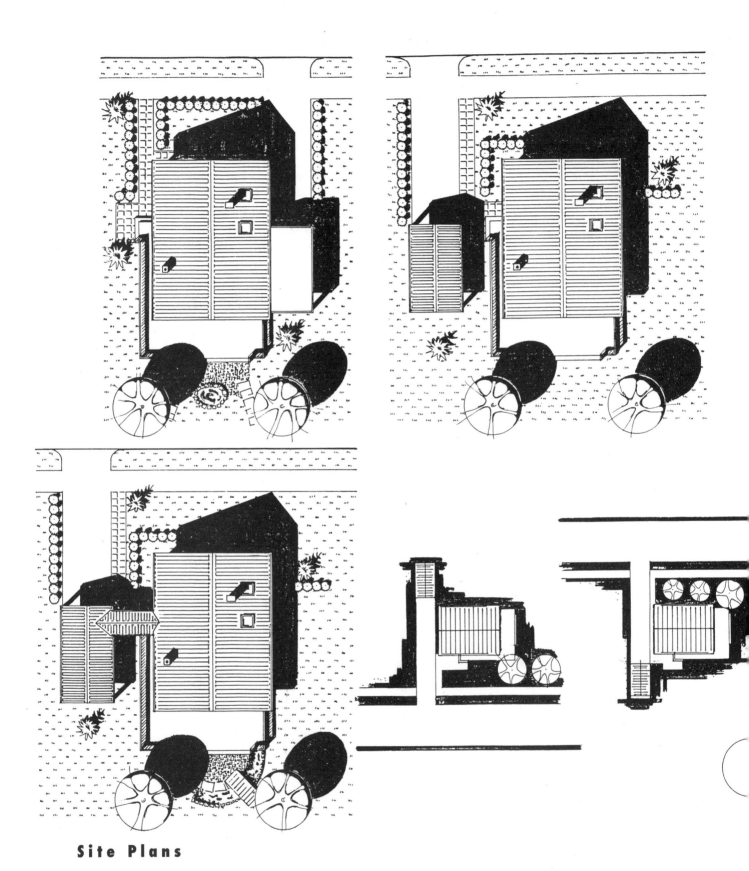

Site Plans

Floor Plans

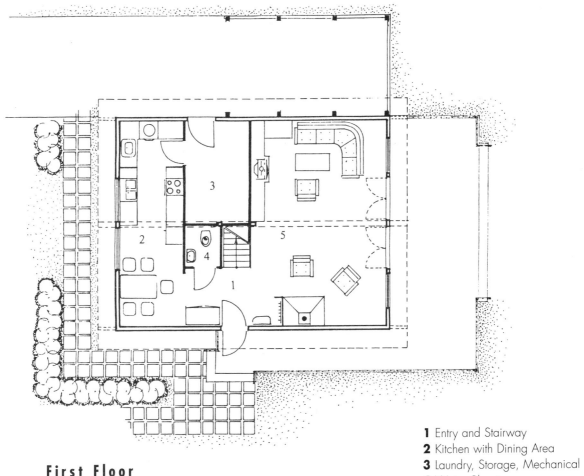

First Floor

1 Entry and Stairway
2 Kitchen with Dining Area
3 Laundry, Storage, Mechanical
4 Water Closet
5 Living Room
6 Hall and Stairway
7 Bedroom
8 Bathroom
9 Bedroom
10 Bedroom

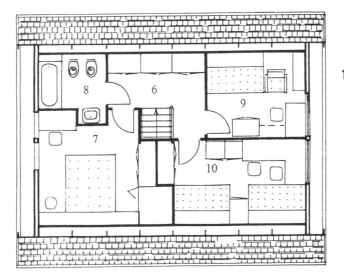

Second Floor

Elevations

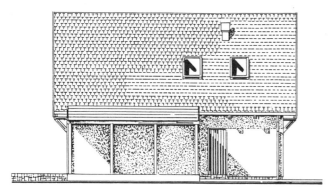

East

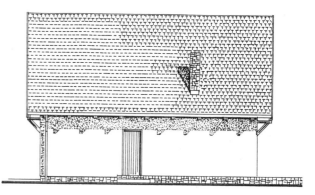

West

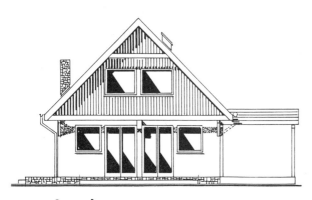

South

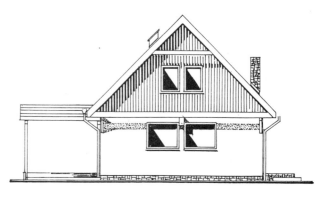

North

Axonometrics

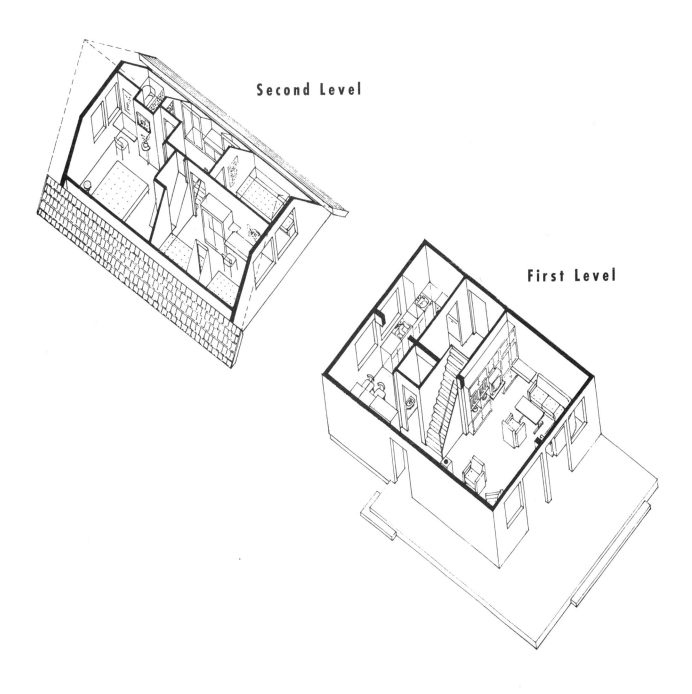

Second Level

First Level

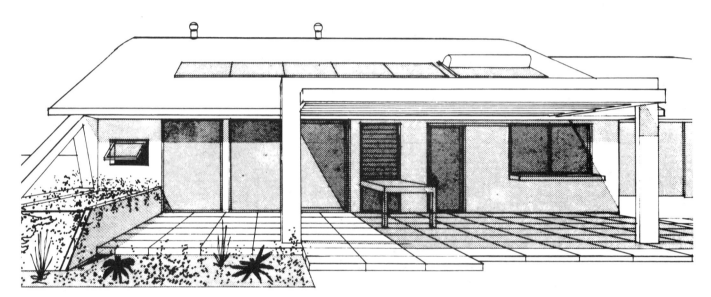

Perspective

SHIPLEY

■ | Jury Comments |

A design that understands sun, shade, and wind. The home appearance fits well with the landscape. The design ably achieves energy efficiency.

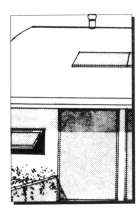

The setting is a large sheep farm in Western Australia where the eldest son is to be married and requires a small house in which to start family life. The region enjoys an abundance of sunshine with a fairly consistent prevailing wind.

The design criteria are (1) to harness the natural elements by positioning solar collectors on the north-facing roof and by installing a wind generator; (2) to provide a cool house in the summer and a warm house in the winter, which in the Southern Hemisphere requires a north-facing orientation; and (3) to create a feeling of space within the limits of a small house.

I set out to achieve a spacious feeling by allowing the attic floor to extend into a mezzanine, with access via a pull-out ladder. The attic space can provide both convenient storage and a recreation area for children during the winter months. The cross-section also allows cross-ventilation during the summer.

Agricultural buildings in Western Australia inspired and influenced this design. The end walls are built with rammed earth. All other walls consist of lightweight steel framing clad internally with plasterboard and externally with cement render and, in some areas, timber cladding. The roof is corrugated steel sheeting, well insulated and with a white finish.

W. I. Shipley

■ | Technical Data |

Gross Square Feet:
1,200

Location:
Rural and semirural areas of Australia

Type:
Steel

Materials:
Steel, plasterboard, cement, rammed earth

Estimated Cost to Build:
$100,000

Estimated Cost to Heat/Cool:
$0, with wood-burning stove

Section

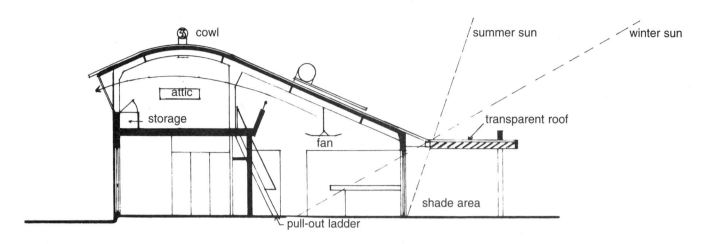

cowl

summer sun

winter sun

attic

storage

transparent roof

fan

shade area

pull-out ladder

Floor Plan

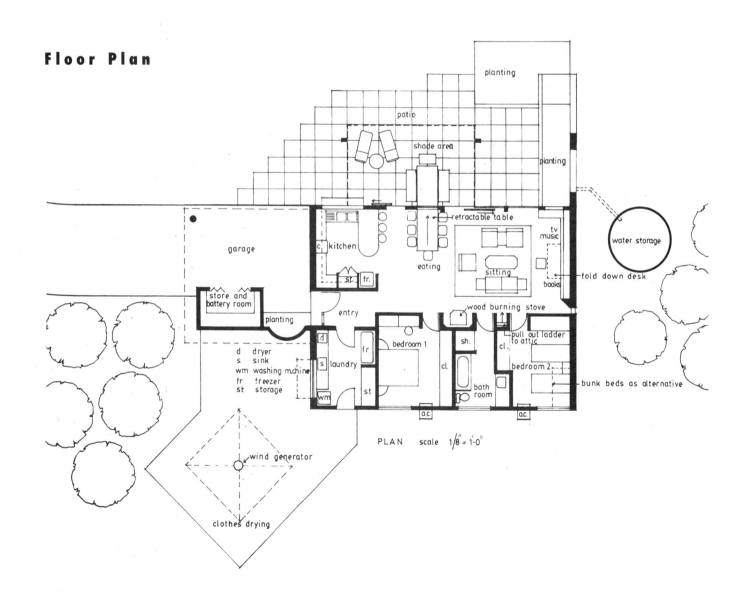

planting

patio

shade area

planting

retractable table

garage

kitchen

c

tv music

water storage

st. fr.

eating

sitting

books

fold down desk

store and battery room

planting

entry

wood burning stove

d

fr

bedroom 1

sh.

cl.

pull out ladder to attic

s

laundry

cl.

bedroom 2

d   dryer
s   sink
wm   washing machine
fr   freezer
st   storage

st

bath room

bunk beds as alternative

wm

a.c.

a.c.

PLAN   scale 1/8" = 1'-0"

wind generator

clothes drying

Elevations

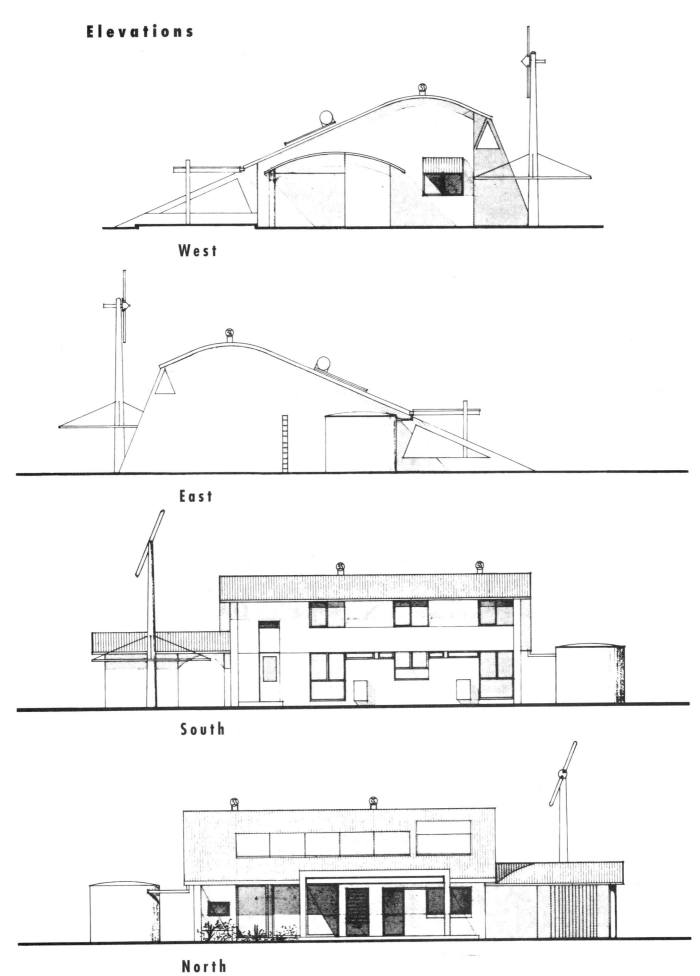

West

East

South

North

Perspective

TAKKEN AND COOPER

■———|Jury Comments|

An effective design for subtropical climates. The house is particularly attuned to the environmental consciousness of the area. Solar considerations and human scale are well understood in this presentation.

A successful form is born of a happy use of materials and emerges as rich as possible in features that reflect its environment. These two dimensions define and demonstrate the deep meaning of architecture.

The compact footprint of this plan enables placement on small lots. With the home sited to take maximum advantage of solar access, the focus of outdoor activity is to the north and east (appropriate to the Southern Hemisphere). Likewise, all living spaces and bedrooms face north and east. Daylight to all spaces eliminates the need for electric lighting during the day. A sloping roof minimizes overshadowing on neighbors and assists smooth airflow over the building to reduce heat loss.

The design groups together all service areas to minimize hot water pipe runs. The house is insulated to higher-than-usual levels. Appropriately sized and shaded windows achieve maximum solar efficiency using timber rather than aluminum window frames. A south-north air path cross-ventilates all spaces. Other energy-efficient and environmentally friendly features include a gas-boosted solar hot water system, compact fluorescent lights, small cisterns for toilets, aerators on water taps, nontoxic termite barriers, and acrylic paints. The structural framing uses plantation timber, while the window frames consist of cladding and recycled timber. Collection of rainwater and pressurized pumping using solar power are key energy features. A covered area outside allows laundry to dry even in wet weather.

Robert Takken and Matthew Cooper

■———|Technical Data|

Gross Square Feet:
1,022

Location:
Brisbane,
Queensland,
Australia

Type:
Wood frame and
aluminum

Materials:
Environmentally
friendly interior
products, aluminum,
plantation and
recycled timber

**Estimated Cost
to Build:**
$62,000

**Estimated Cost to
Heat/Cool:**
$0

Site and Floor Plans

1 Gatehouse
2 Carpet
3 Storage
4 Rainwater Tanks
5 Entry
6 Dining
7 Kitchen
8 Living Room
9 Deck
10 Laundry
11 Courtyard
12 Bathroom
13 Bedroom 2
14 Bedroom 1
15 Solar Collectors

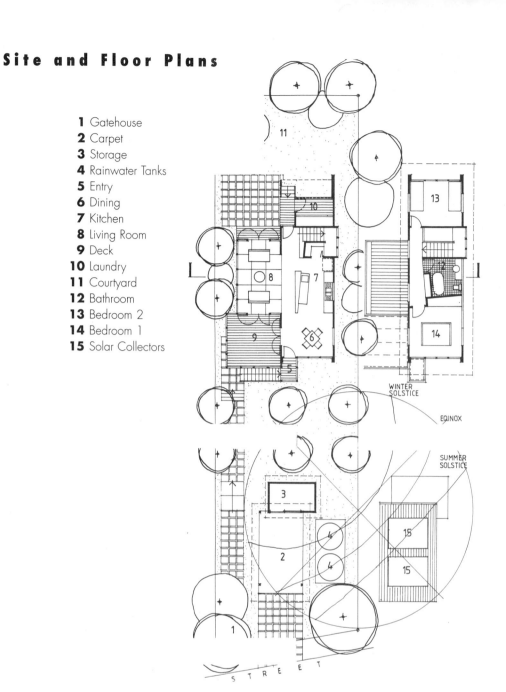

West Elevation

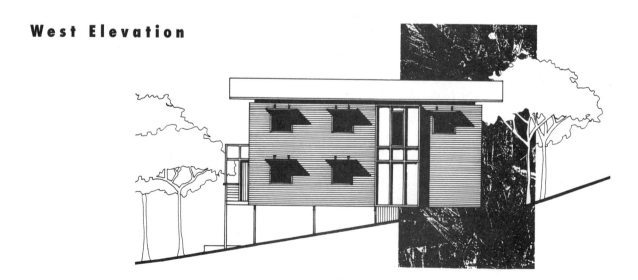

Axonometric

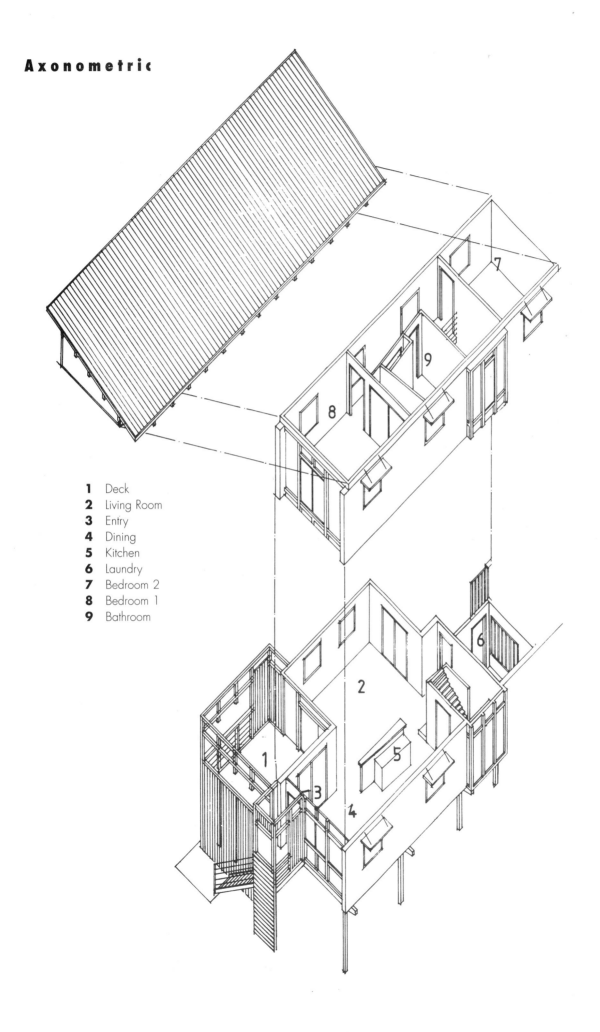

1 Deck
2 Living Room
3 Entry
4 Dining
5 Kitchen
6 Laundry
7 Bedroom 2
8 Bedroom 1
9 Bathroom

Perspective

FABBRI

■— Jury Comments

A unique and elegant solution to the design of a small house. The architecture is presented as sculpture. The floor plan has both unusual and practical elements, such as locating the bedrooms over the garage while configuring the other areas of the house in one long wing. The proposed landscaping is very European.

This small home embodies a space that is no less beautiful or elegant than a larger home. The landscape and the building form a geometrical design, but the asymmetry of the house and the separation into autonomous parts give movement to the complex. The building consists of two different blocks: a low, long, linear element and, opposite, the massive element of the tower. In the linear part, the day area — an open space only interrupted by the chimney — separates the living room from the dining area.

The main axis of the plan goes through the sheet of water in front of the house, passes through the home, and stops at the semicircular fountain fed by a little brook. That solution extends the perception of interior space, which directly communicates with the exterior, as encouraged by the glass doors that face the porticos.

As far as energy savings are concerned, the house has solar panels on the tower roof, which consists of lamellate (layered) wood; a chimney with boiler system connected to the heating system; a serpentine solar hot water heater under the grass; and a cooling system that takes advantage of the sheet of water in front of the house.

The design is conceived for a flat site. The home stands out in an ornate landscape inspired by the geometry of Renaissance gardens.

Giulio Fabbri

■— Technical Data

Gross Square Feet:
1,180

Location:
Italy; a flat, solitary site in the country

Type:
Brick with wooden beam flooring

Materials:
Brick and local stone on exterior, plaster, wood for the roof of the tower and copper for the low building, local stone for interior walls, marble for the floors, lacunar (cavitated) ceilings of recessed tiles

Estimated Cost to Build:
$250,000

Estimated Cost to Heat/Cool:
$2,500 per year

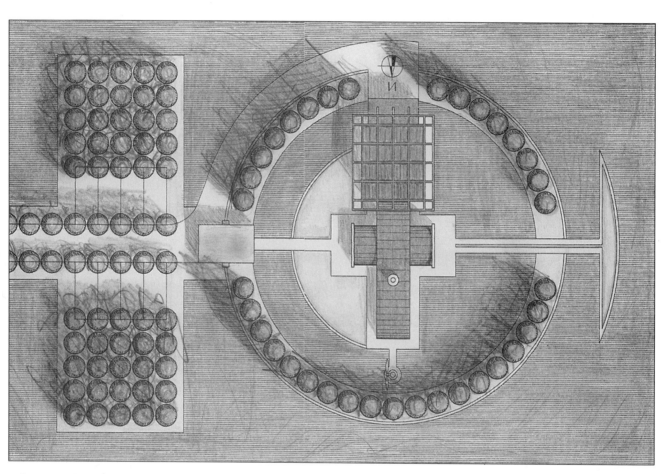

Site Plan

Floor Plans

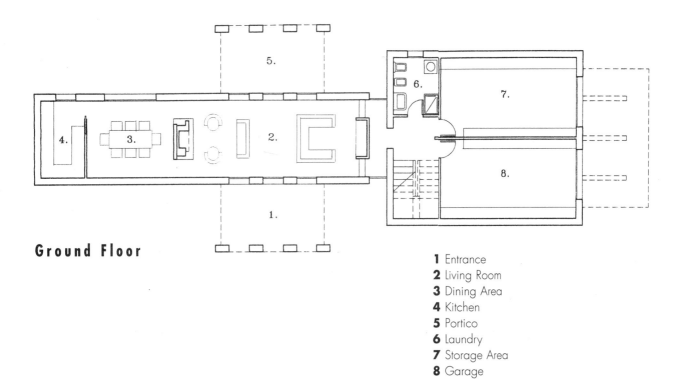

Ground Floor

Upper Floor

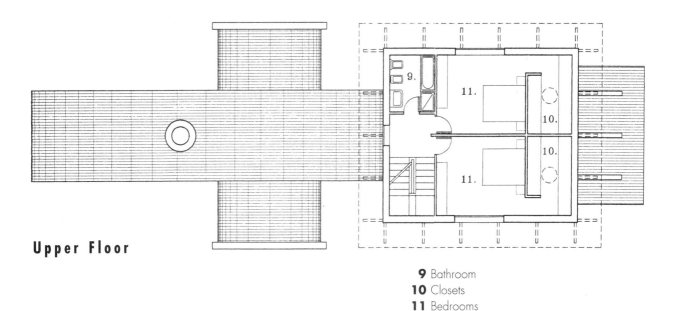

1 Entrance
2 Living Room
3 Dining Area
4 Kitchen
5 Portico
6 Laundry
7 Storage Area
8 Garage

9 Bathroom
10 Closets
11 Bedrooms

Elevations

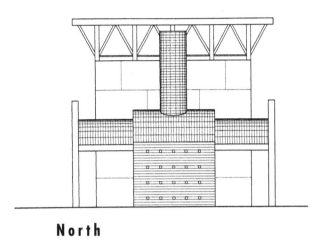

North

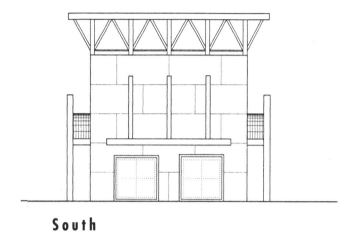

South

West

Axonometrics

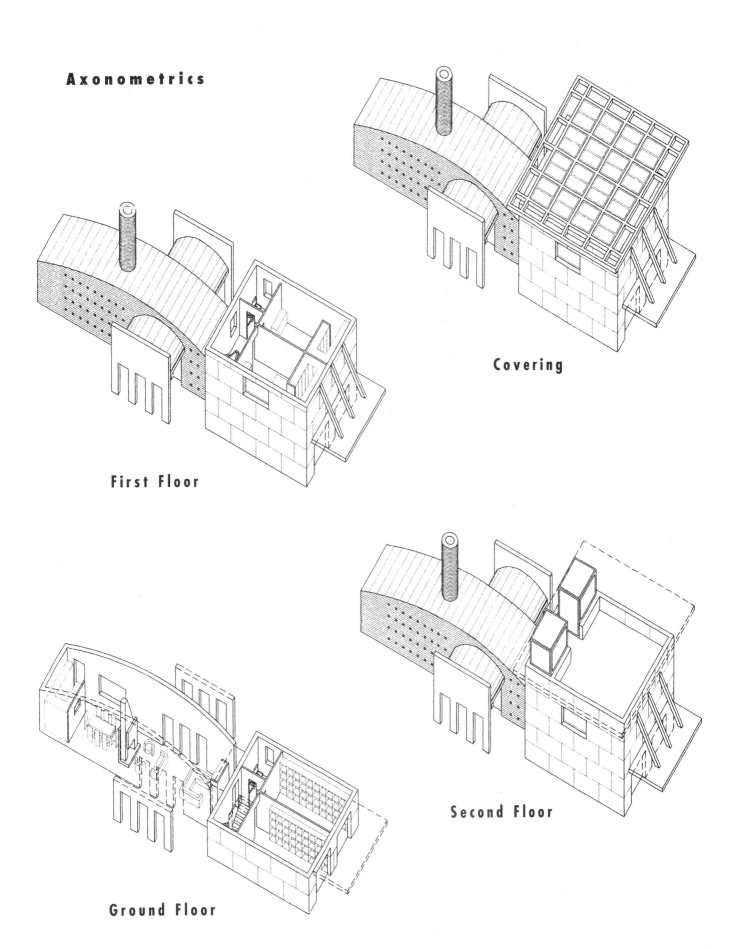

Covering

First Floor

Second Floor

Ground Floor

Perspective

GIULIANI

Jury Comments

A wonderfully imaginative design in the best contemporary tradition. Monumental characteristics, such as the entry stairway, are scaled to a compact design. An exciting use of exterior geometry to complement the interior.

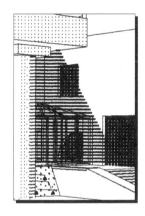

This house has two functional floors: one for the living areas and the other for resting and studying. The ground floor includes the dining and lounge areas with adjacent kitchen and conservatory, as well as a laundry and a storeroom that contains the main plant and systems. The double volume of the entrance lounge incorporates a circular wooden staircase that connects the two levels. At ground level is a box garage.

On the upper floor are the spaces for study and work, and a separate night area — two bedrooms with half baths. This level also has a full bathroom as well as a stairway leading to the terrace.

The construction technique employs reinforced concrete frame and curtain walls. Inside, gypsum walls and an insulation layer create a heat-cold barrier. The flooring consists of polished lime and fired terracotta powder. The external window and door frames are in copper and zinc alloy. Lime plaster and marble sawdust cover the outside walls, while copper sheets cover the roof.

Carlo Giuliani

Technical Data

Gross Square Feet:
1,250

Location:
Italy

Type:
Concrete construction

Materials:
Concrete, gypsum, copper, zinc

Estimated Cost to Build:
$200,000

Estimated Cost to Heat/Cool:
$1,600 per year

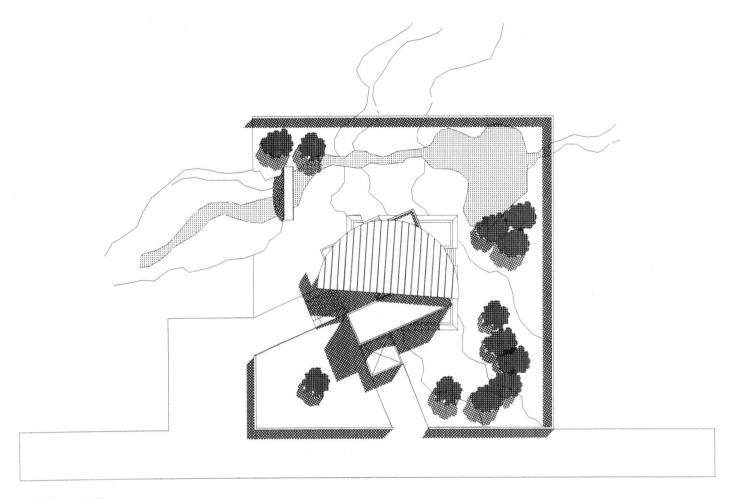

Site Plan

Floor Plans

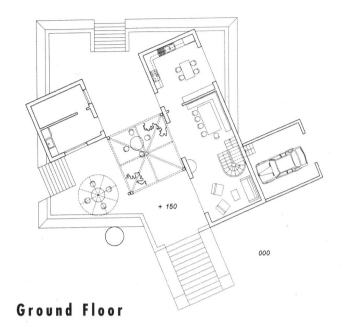

+ 150

000

Ground Floor

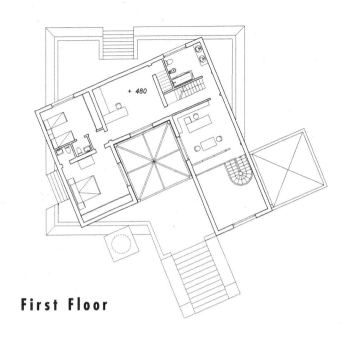

+ 480

First Floor

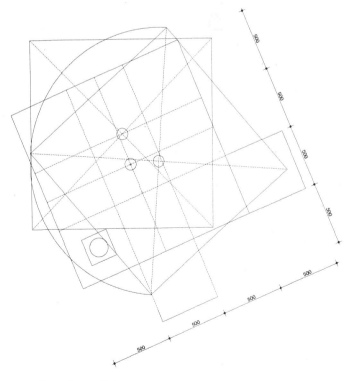

500
500
500
500
500
500
500
500

Design Diagram

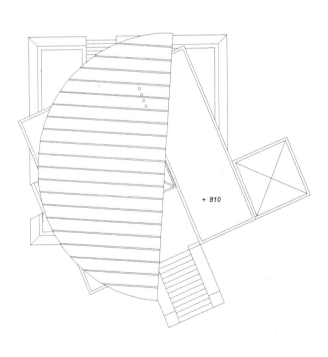

+ 810

Roof

Elevations

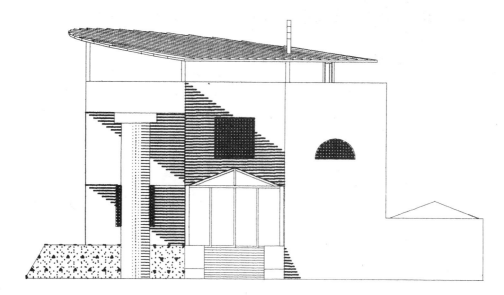

Northeast

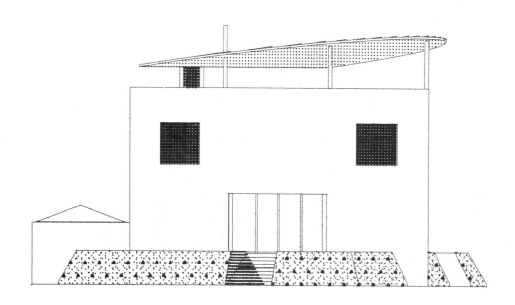

Southwest

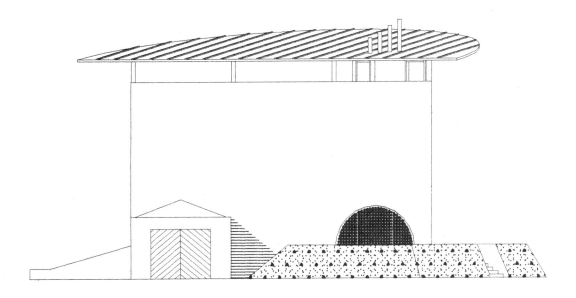

Northwest

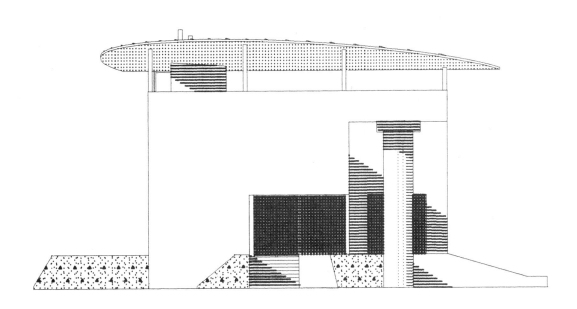

Southeast

Perspective

HELLUM

A straightforward design with no frills. The west elevation has a particularly strong aesthetic. A separate carport helps to expand space visually. An interesting focus of the design is improved indoor air quality, partially provided by an interior garden.

The design focuses on providing a clean indoor environment for the occupants of this house. A living indoor garden produces oxygen and helps to filter indoor air pollutants. Mechanically operated blinds between the glass in the garden walls regulate heat transmission. A tank in the ground or under the house stores fresh water for occupants and plants.

A heat exchanger in the loft replaces used air with outside air. Air intake from the roof is distributed to the garden area, partly through soil ventilation. In this way the garden serves as a fresh-air filter. When designing the garden, it is important to select plants that are resistant to low temperatures and to choose plant nutrients that do not adversely affect human living conditions.

The house design provides for privacy, a view outdoors from the kitchen, controlled traffic areas inside and outside, and direct access from the living area to the garden. The possibility exists for future expansion.

Ulrik Hellum

Technical Data

Gross Square Feet:
1,008

Location:
Norway; other cold climates

Type:
Wood frame

Materials:
Wood roof and walls, tiled concrete for ground floor

Estimated Cost to Build:
$80,000

Estimated Cost to Heat/Cool:
Approximately 30 percent lower than comparable housing

Floor Plans

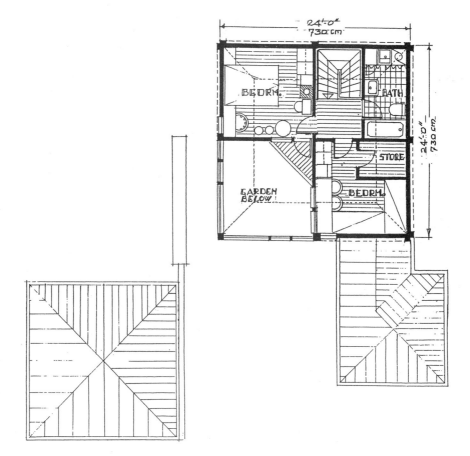

24'-0"
730 cm

BEDRM.

BATH

24'-0"
730 cm.

STORE

GARDEN
BELOW

BEDRM.

First Floor

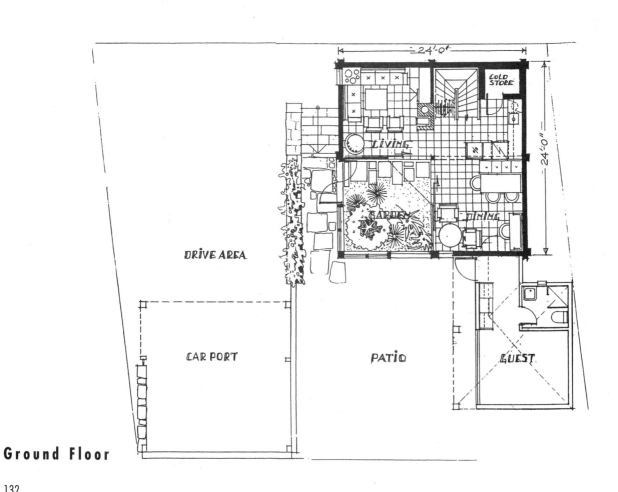

24'-0"

COLD
STORE

24'-0"

LIVING

DRIVE AREA

GARDEN

DINING

CAR PORT

PATIO

GUEST

Ground Floor

Elevations

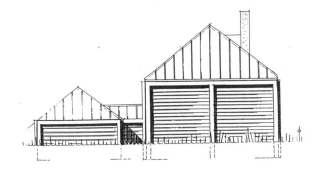

East

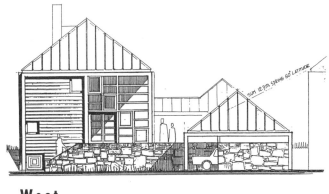

West

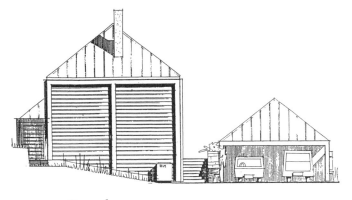

North

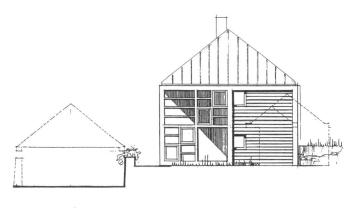

South

Perspective

KEANE & KEANE

Jury Comments

An imaginative team-designed small house that is especially well suited to a rural or forest site. The home has an attractive exterior and an open, functional interior with a kitchen overlooking the large deck.

Based on the client profile, we develop residential architectural images: aesthetically, functionally, and financially. We then educate the client to create an architectural awareness and a collaborative process of design elaboration. Thus, our major influences are the client, the site, and the budget.

For this house design, a recently retired couple bought a beautiful piece of land and wished to build their dream home overlooking a small kettle (a glacial depression) that dominates the site. A tight budget produced a simple volume with three zones: the garage/service area, the great-room/entertainment-living area, and the bedroom area. The intent was to create apparent grandeur out of a modest

plan. This led to the great room's steeply sloped roof, which is the key feature of the home. The slope of the roof also affords secondary overflow space for the couple's periodic visits from extended family members.

The home is oriented toward the kettle, with a substantial deck projecting out into the landscape. This zone in the site also creates a natural pocket, with the home set to the far western edge of the lot. The great room anchors the visual axis from east to west through the greatest interior volume of the home. Heavy timber beams span this space to reinforce the woods environment of this property in southeastern Wisconsin.

Mark Keane and Linda Keane

Technical Data

Gross Square Feet:
1,250

Location:
Jackson, Wisconsin

Type:
Wood frame

Materials:
Cedar siding, heavy timber members, asphalt shingle roofing

Estimated Cost to Build:
$120,000

Estimated Cost to Heat/Cool:
$1,400 per year

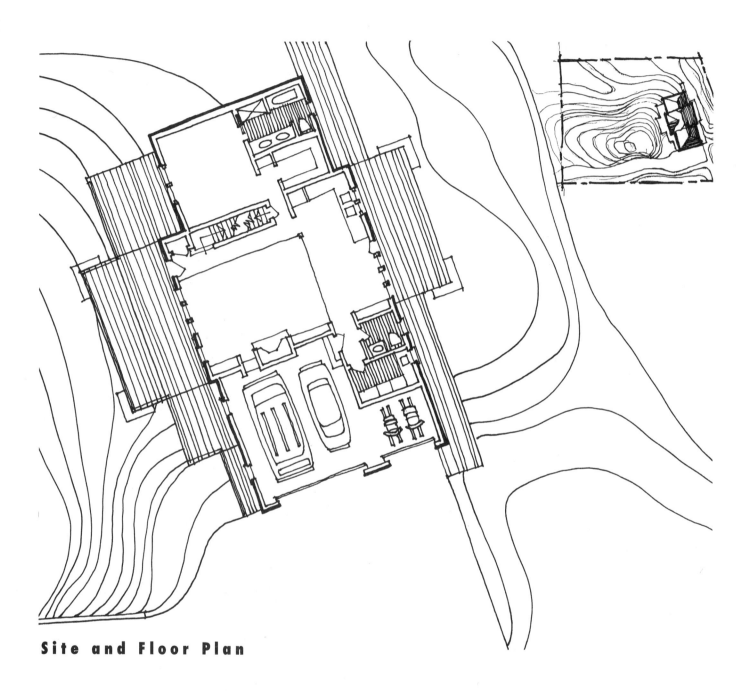

Site and Floor Plan

West Elevation

Section

East Elevation

Great Room Axonometric

Perspective

LUTHER

■ Jury Comments

One of the best environment- and energy-conscious designs in this competition. Specific analysis and attention to all of the geographic and building considerations. Attractive design and attention to sustainable design concepts.

Architecture should represent the simplicity of space through its function, aesthetics, and comfort. When we correctly integrate technology with the design, we achieve an architecture responsive to our environment. We should expect our architecture, as with any other commodity we use, to provide us with the best quality, performance, and efficiency possible.

The objective of this design is to promote a sustainable living environment within the requirements of a small house. These requirements include passive solar design, efficient and economical use of building materials, and a garden for produce and compost. Such features strengthen and become an integral part of a small house design. Flexible and adaptable space echoes the concept of sustainability.

This design incorporates a hybrid mechanical system. Passive solar heating and cooling combine with the radiant-hydronic floor system and conventional ceiling ventilation fans. Solar hot water integrates with the hydronic heating system. The central stairwell produces negative air pressure at the cupola, enhancing natural ventilation.

An innovative structural system employs highly insulated stress-skin panels. These panels not only reduce by about 60 percent the consumption of timber when compared to conventional housing, but conserve energy as well. A lightweight, ventilated metal roof, insulated at the ceiling, helps reduce summer cooling loads. The assembly of this modular system allows for easy future additions.

Mark B. Luther

■ Technical Data

Gross Square Feet:
1,080

Location:
Melbourne, Australia

Type:
Modular construction

Materials:
Wood, metal, stress-skin panels

Estimated Cost to Build:
N/A

Estimated Cost to Heat/Cool:
N/A

Site and Floor Plans

Site

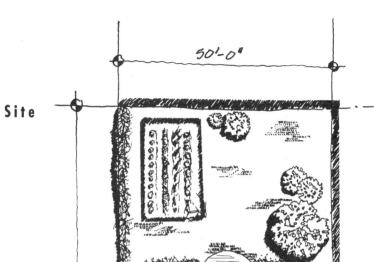

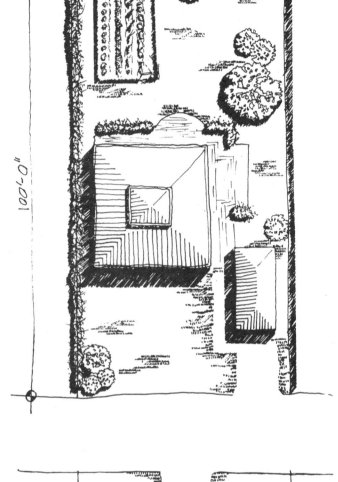

50'-0"

100'-0"

First Floor

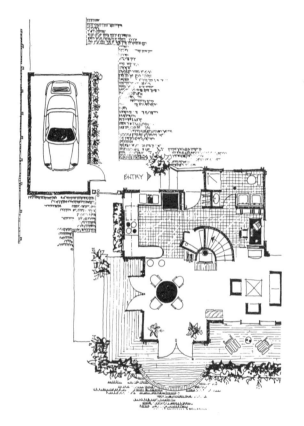

ENTRY

Second Floor

Elevations

East

North

South

West

Axonometrics

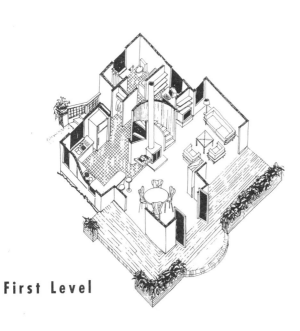

First Level

Second Level

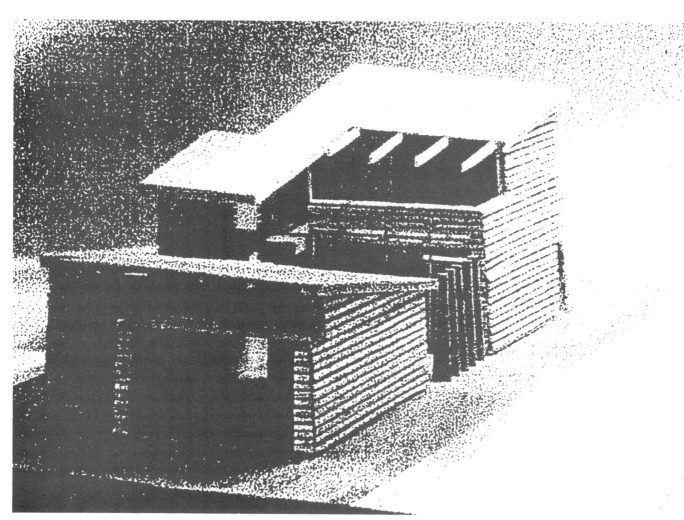

Perspective

STUDIO OF PACIFIC ARCHITECTURE

■—| Jury Comments |

A practical, elongated design that would work nicely in a confined urban landscape. The interior, from a physical/functional standpoint, is particularly well suited to the design. An environmentally conscious design.

This "Eco House" seeks to discover innovative construction techniques that are both ecologically and environmentally sound, and at the same time searches for an appropriate aesthetic to give meaningful expression to the demands of contemporary city living.

We chose an extremely simple and flexible plan, organized around a garden patio in the form of two pavilions connected by a glazed walkway. From a poetical and ecological stance, the garden patio is the essential filter and focus for the house: cool in summer and warm in winter. The patio, open to the sky, is bounded on the western side by a delicate vertical garden, which acts as a screen to filter the sun, offers protection from the wind, and provides a visual barrier that can be modified to suit the occupants' needs. The patio could be partially or completely covered at a later date. The plan arrangement allows occupants to look through spaces, creating visual delight and adding spatial depth to what is essentially a very small house.

The design satisfies the need for environmental sensitivity by maximizing insulation to reduce winter heat loss and summer heat gain; by relying on solar energy to reduce space-heating requirements; and by using materials that derive from sustainable sources, that require minimum energy consumption in both construction and manufacture, and that come from the local economy. The design allows for possible expansion as well as for flexibility in adapting spaces for different purposes as occupants' needs change over time.

Studio of Pacific Architecture

■—| Technical Data |

Gross Square Feet:
1,197

Location:
Newtown, Wellington, New Zealand

Type:
Wood frame

Materials:
Plywood box beams for structural framework, rock wool insulation, concrete flooring, recycled products

Estimated Cost to Build:
$72,000

Estimated Cost to Heat/Cool:
N/A

Floor Plans

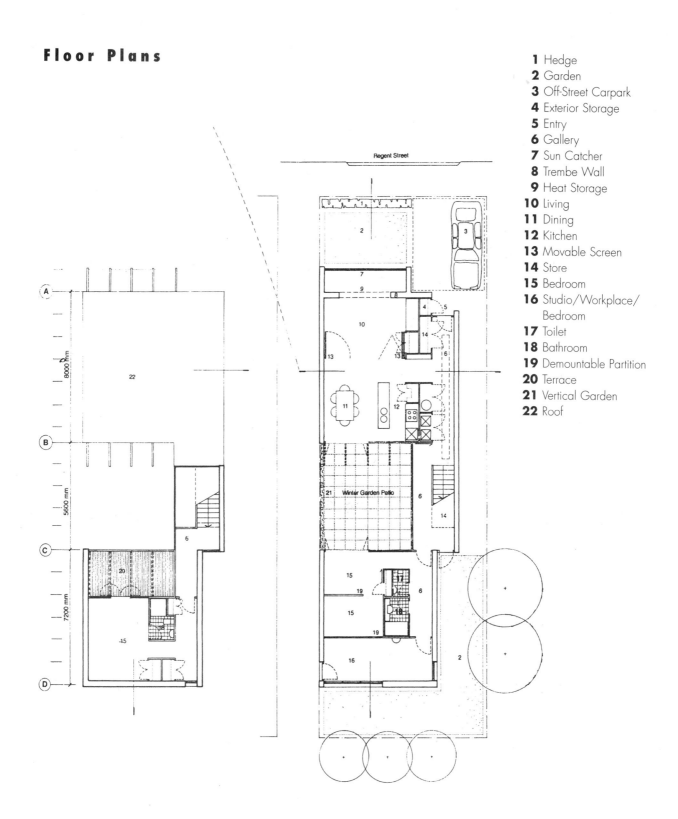

1 Hedge
2 Garden
3 Off-Street Carpark
4 Exterior Storage
5 Entry
6 Gallery
7 Sun Catcher
8 Trembe Wall
9 Heat Storage
10 Living
11 Dining
12 Kitchen
13 Movable Screen
14 Store
15 Bedroom
16 Studio/Workplace/
Bedroom
17 Toilet
18 Bathroom
19 Demountable Partition
20 Terrace
21 Vertical Garden
22 Roof

Regent Street

Winter Garden Patio

Upper Floor   **Ground Floor**

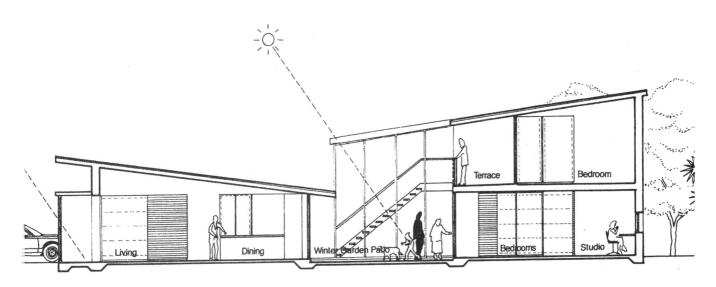

Section

Living   Dining   Winter Garden Patio   Terrace   Bedroom   Bedrooms   Studio

Perspective

BUOEN

An exciting floor plan that, via a unique entryway, allows one to enter various areas without disturbing other areas. Nice integration of the yard, garage, and activity areas. A visually attractive design.

My proposal is a design that will fit into existing neighborhoods while providing a comfortable, compact, and efficient environment. A gracious entry disperses traffic to the various living spaces, obviating any need to pass through other areas of the house. The exterior not only accommodates outdoor activities, but also offers views from the interior, making the small house appear larger. On the street side of the property, a front porch allows for relaxed viewing.

Energy efficiency is a primary concern in the design, from the orientation of the plan to the use of appropriate construction materials. The design specifies masonry walls with a 6-inch superinsulation system and large roof overhangs with extensive

insulation in the attic. The air-conditioning and heating system consists of a closed-loop, ground-source heat pump, using a deep-well concept for the heat exchanger. This prevents equipment damage due to exposure to the elements, eliminates the need to hide the equipment with landscaping, and reduces noise pollution.

This house design takes visual advantage of the surroundings. A short driveway connects the carport or garage to the street. A small basement provides inside storage, space for mechanical equipment, and a laundry area.

Don Buoen

Technical Data

Gross Square Feet:
1,248

Location:
Oklahoma and other
U.S. central states

Type:
Wood frame

Materials:
2 x 6 stud wall with
masonry veneer exterior, standing-seam
metal roofing, slate
tile flooring, painted
sheetrock or wallpapered walls

**Estimated Cost
to Build:**
$100,000

**Estimated Cost to
Heat/Cool:**
$450 per year

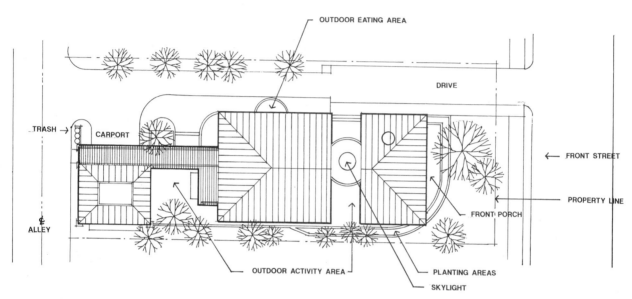

OUTDOOR EATING AREA

DRIVE

TRASH →

CARPORT

← FRONT STREET

← PROPERTY LINE

℄ ALLEY

FRONT PORCH

OUTDOOR ACTIVITY AREA

PLANTING AREAS

SKYLIGHT

Site Plan

Floor Plans

Basement

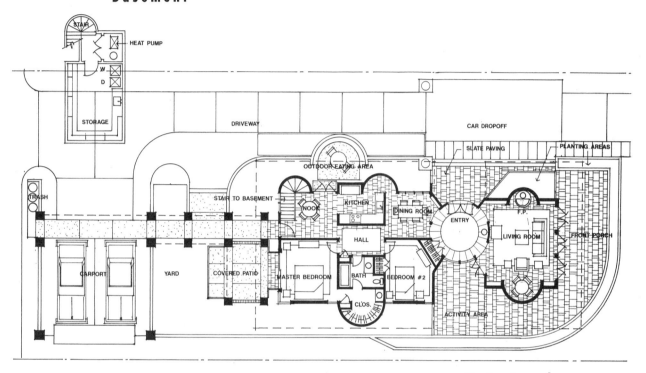

STAIR

HEAT PUMP

W

D

STORAGE

DRIVEWAY

CAR DROPOFF

SLATE PAVING

PLANTING AREAS

OUTDOOR EATING AREA

TRASH

STAIR TO BASEMENT

NOOK

KITCHEN

DINING ROOM

ENTRY

F.P.

LIVING ROOM

FRONT PORCH

HALL

CARPORT

YARD

COVERED PATIO

MASTER BEDROOM

BATH

BEDROOM #2

CL'OS.

ACTIVITY AREA

Main Level

Elevations

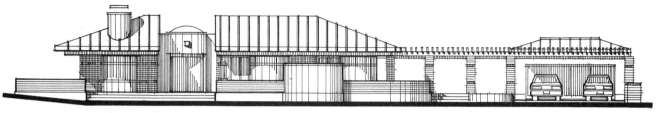

North

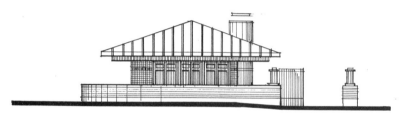

East

South

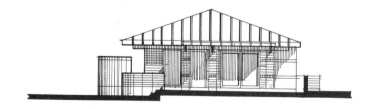

West

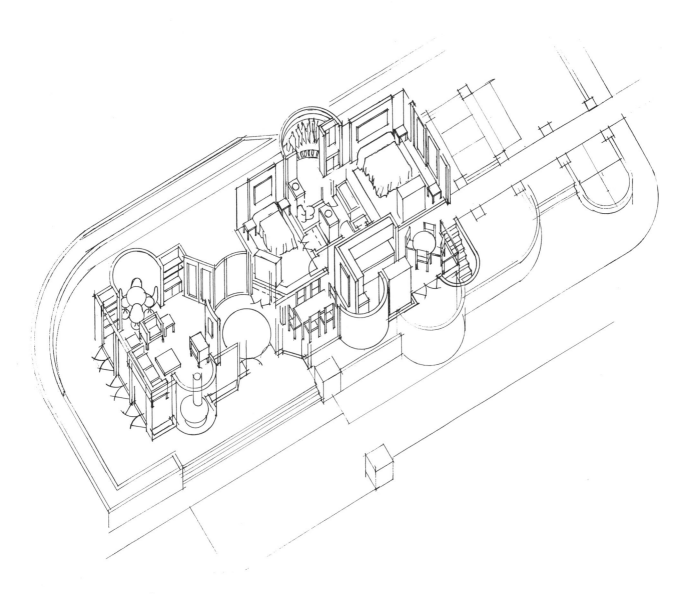

Axonometric

Perspective

FAORO

Interesting typology and mixture of scales and elements give the illusion of greater space. The floor plan is particularly attractive. The design does a good job connecting the interior to the outdoors.

Designed to be visually and spatially appealing, and intended for clients who can afford larger homes, this small residence includes features for changing lifestyles: a home office with a private entry (which can be used as a third bedroom), and a lower-level interior atrium space for a family theater. The design incorporates privacy gradients and a half-hidden garden, bedrooms with east light, and sheltering roofs. The split-level layout stresses integration with the landscape through the use of a courtyard, focused views, and transitional spaces. A front porch places emphasis on the public realm of the street and encourages neighborhood supervision.

The design visually enhances the exterior dimensions by using saddlebags and dormers and by repeating building forms as outbuildings in the landscape. Placing the garage in profile, as seen from the street,

minimizes its visual impact and adds to the frontal aspect of the house. Open planning in the living/dining/kitchen, combined with raised ceiling areas, increases the sense of interior space. A central entry and stairway minimize unnecessary circulation.

The form reflects the climate in several ways. Earth berms elongate the east-west axis, and minimal openings face the north and east. Large glazed areas on the west and south take advantage of passive solar gain, with foliage for seasonal shading. The lower level is partially below grade to conserve energy. Other energy-related features include superinsulation in the walls (R-25) and roof (R-50), minimal air infiltration, use of natural light, low-E glass, blinds between the window panes on the south and west, and an energy-efficient, 40-gallon, on-demand water heater.

Daniel L. Faoro

Gross Square Feet:
1,250

Location:
North Dakota; suited to Midwest/North Central United States

Type:
Wood frame

Materials:
Environmentally appropriate materials, such as engineered recyclable wood and structural insulated panels; vinyl siding

Estimated Cost to Build:
$75,000

Estimated Cost to Heat/Cool:
80 percent lower than comparable houses

Site and Floor Plans

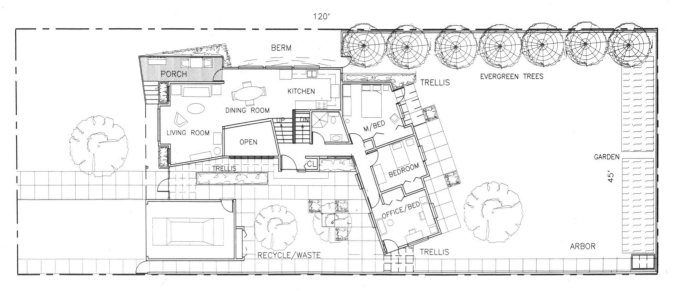

Site and Ground Floor

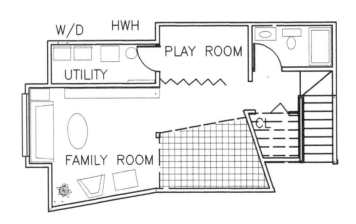

Lower Level

Elevations

North

East

South

West

Axonometric

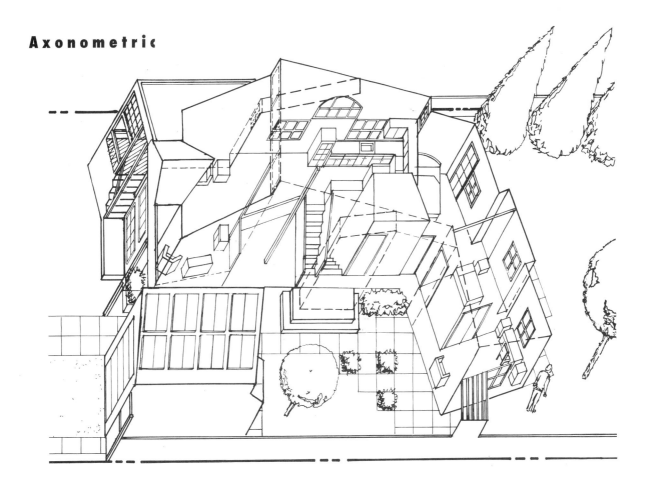

Perspective

HAIDER & AZHAR

■ Jury Comments

A family-oriented small home for growth and change. Sited for natural solar gain. Decking provides flexible use. Solar orientation is used to reduce energy costs.

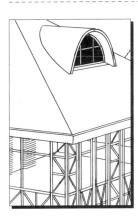

Designed for a young and growing family, this split-level enables easy adaptation of the interior to changing family circumstances. Knowledge of how young people dwell inside their homes — plus an understanding of movement, light, spaciousness, and how to create attractive areas for relaxation or children's play — contributes integrally to the concept.

The vertical spatial hierarchy of the open plan is easy to modify with minimal architectural intervention. The living, dining, and kitchen areas and the spaces around the central staircase collectively form one large continuum that permits multiple uses. The covered deck and the walk-up attic also provide additional living space for the future. The articulated spaces create a visually connected and dramatic interior environment — both horizontally and vertically — especially for children.

This particular design takes advantage of a 5-foot drop toward the middle of the site, but can be easily modified to effectively accommodate a half-raised or walk-out basement on a flat site. The covered deck or terrace, which overlooks a picturesque park across the street, provides a safe play area for children and can be either screened or left open.

The design addresses energy savings and environmental concerns primarily through orientation, with the majority of the windows facing southeast or southwest. Insulation and proper ventilation devices help to create an energy-efficient home.

Jawaid Haider and Talat Azhar

■ Technical Data

Gross Square Feet:
1,250

Location:
Central Pennsylvania, but adaptable to other areas

Type:
Wood frame split-level

Materials:
Wood frame construction on a 3-foot, 6-inch grid; external vinyl siding; double-insulated vinyl windows; metal; brick

Estimated Cost to Build:
$100,000

Estimated Cost to Heat/Cool:
$700 per year

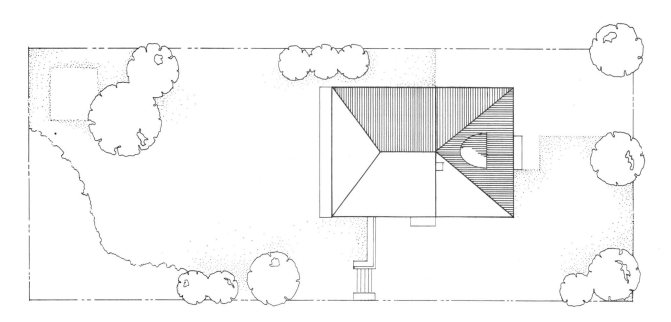

Site Plan

Floor Plans

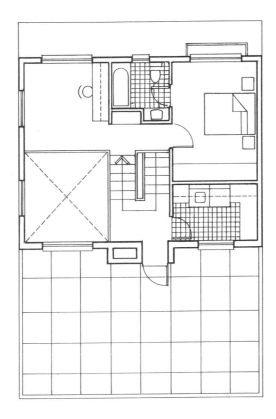

Levels 1 and 2

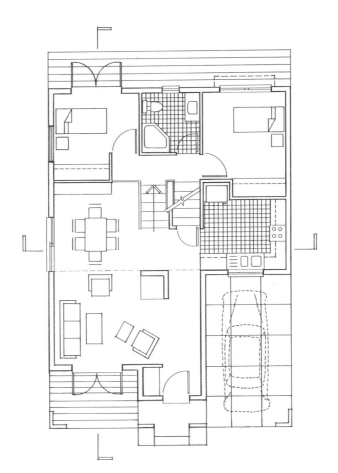

Levels 3 and 4

Elevations

Northeast

Southwest

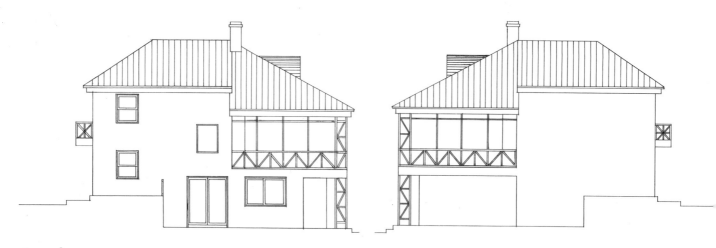

Southeast

Northwest

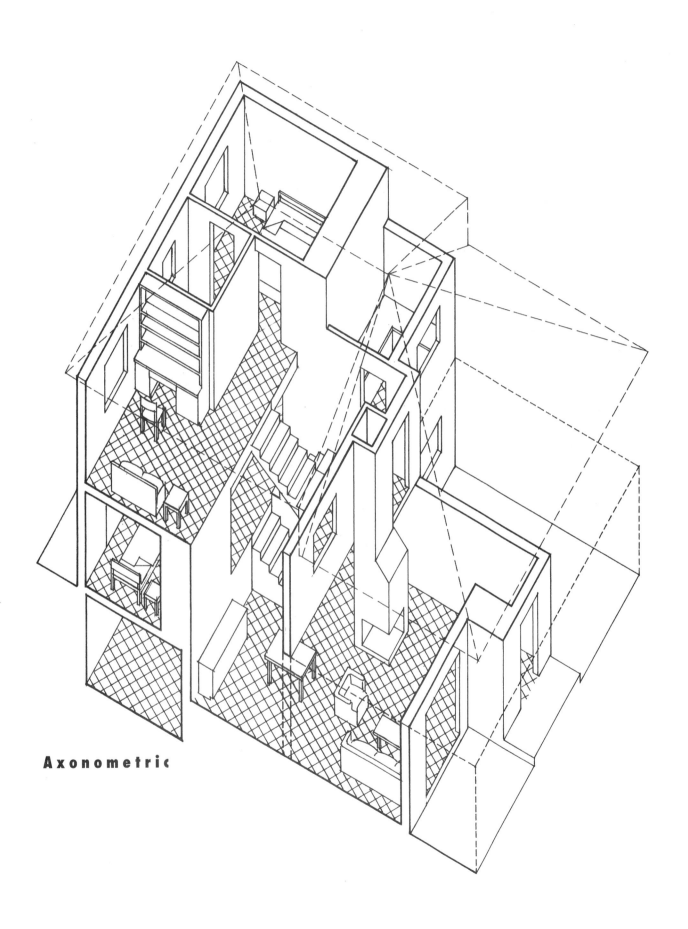

Axonometric

Perspective

SHINDELUS

■─── Jury Comments

A modular, prefabricated concept that will fit the needs of a variety of clients and geographical locations. Expandable and pleasing.

This design consists of a small prefab modular house with integrated passive solar heating, solar power, and solar hot water, thereby allowing homeowners to reduce the amount of income spent on basic shelter. The prefab house is versatile, offering the owners and builders elevation, material, and plan variations to produce a "custom" house.

The concept arranges four modules, each 13 x 24 feet, so as to capture a basement (12 x 23 feet) and a passive solar sunroom (13 x 18 feet), the latter featuring a prefab greenhouse that closes the southernmost wall. Metal module trusses (floor joist, studs, and roof rafters screwed together) slide into

and bolt into two 24-foot-long metal channel beams with sleeves at 24 inches on center. The builders add metal blocking, plate straps, and so on, before attaching plywood sheeting, windows, and exterior materials.

The finished modules, set by crane and sealed, anchor the site-built garage and patio covers. The insulated thermal-mass slab, combined with built-in sliding window insulation work, delays temperature fluctuation and reduces the need for air conditioning.

Bruce Shindelus

■─── Technical Data

Gross Square Feet:
1,248

Location:
Cold but sunny areas in the United States, such as Colorado

Type:
Modular

Materials:
Metal frame; exterior finish could be wood, masonite, cement board, or stucco

Estimated Cost to Build:
$50,000

Estimated Cost to Heat/Cool:
33 percent lower than comparable housing

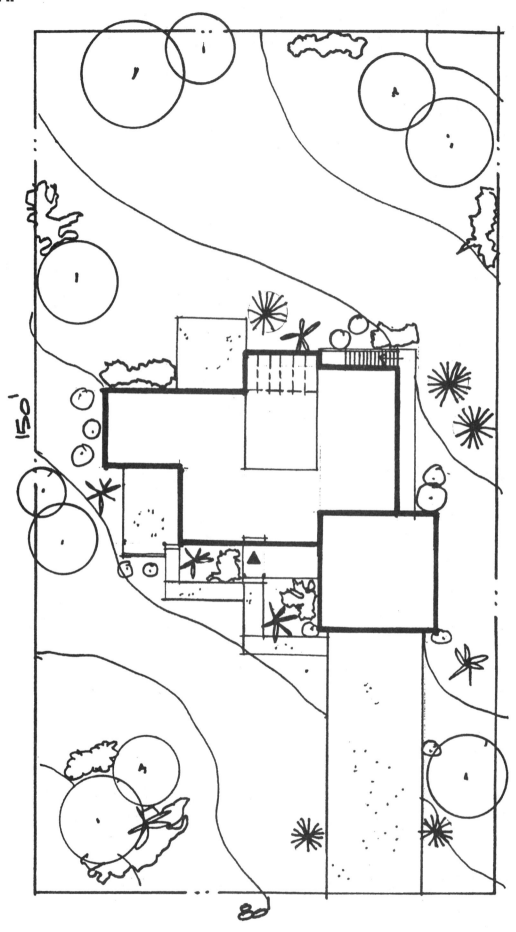

150'

80'

Floor Plans

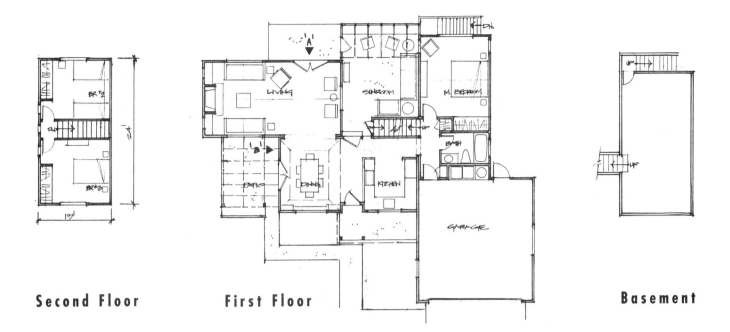

Second Floor **First Floor** **Basement**

Elevations

West **South**

East **North**

Perspective

SYNTHESIS ARCHITECTS

■ Jury Comments

A well-conceived design with attention to the human–building–environment interface. Adaptable to a variety of sites. Energy efficient and otherwise environmentally conscious.

We knew we had rare clients when they stated in a letter they wanted a perfectly round door. They were committed to capitalizing on nature's earth-sheltering and solar-gain capabilities, utilizing a Clivus Multrum composting toilet with graywater filtration systems, and heating with a central Russian-style masonry fireplace.

The architects' ideas translated into an exposed concrete facade with rusticated joints, rough wood-grain patterns, and exposed form-ties. An accent band of earth-toned ceramic tiles above and below the windows and a custom redwood sunscreen add color and depth to the facade. Natural Adirondack bluestone, available on site, is incorporated in the design facade, at the retaining wing walls, in the monitor projections through the earth roof, and as an accent at the vestibule wall with the circular door opening.

The southern exposure of this facade illuminates the interior through large expanses of glass. The windows allow light to enter deep within the building, eliminating the impression of an uninviting hole and creating a warm, sunlit home. The sunscreen is designed to shade the harsh summer sun while welcoming the winter's rays.

Another design feature is a central chimney structure that contains the flue for the Russian fireplace as well as plumbing, kitchen, and mechanical penetrations. We also incorporated the intake and exhaust air from the air-to-air heat exchanger that was required for improved indoor air quality. Conceived in an effort to reduce roof penetrations, this chimney and its symbolic heat source, and the adjacent skylight monitors, illuminate the darker areas of the "underground den" while punctuating the unsuspecting south-facing slope in the Adirondack Mountains.

Synthesis Architects

■ Technical Data

Gross Square Feet:
1,250

Location:
Adirondack Park,
New York

Type:
One story, earth sheltered, passive solar heated

Materials:
Concrete, steel, wood, ceramic tile, bluestone, aluminum

Estimated Cost to Build:
$220,000

Estimated Cost to Heat/Cool:
$250 per year

167

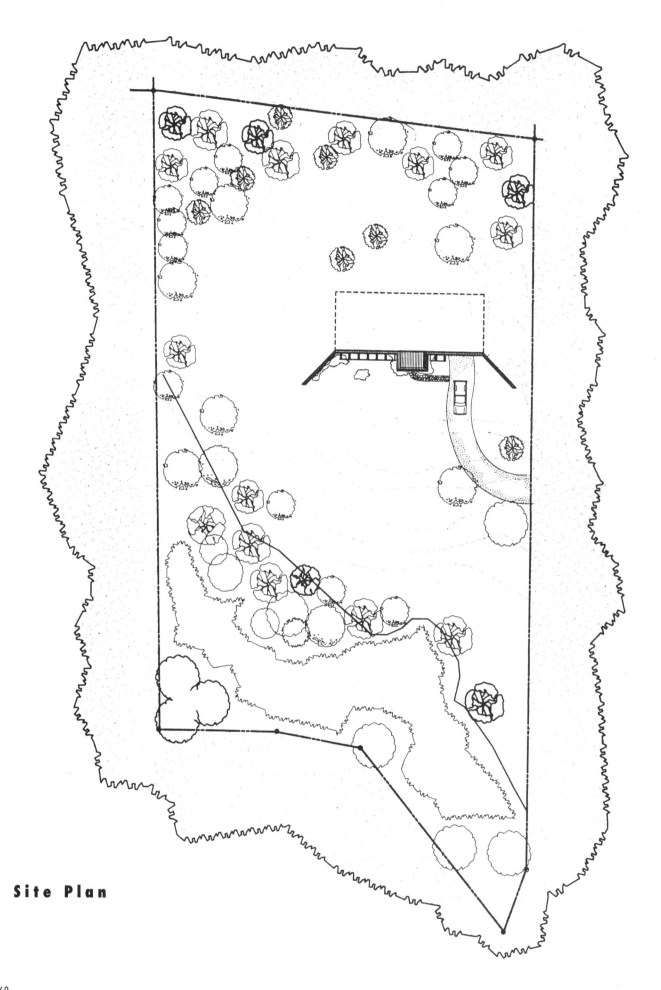

Site Plan

South Elevation

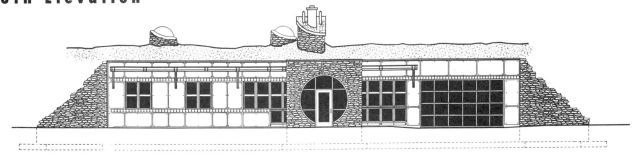

Floor Plan

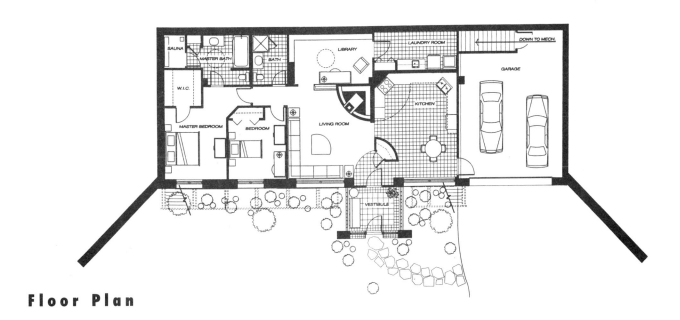

Axonometric

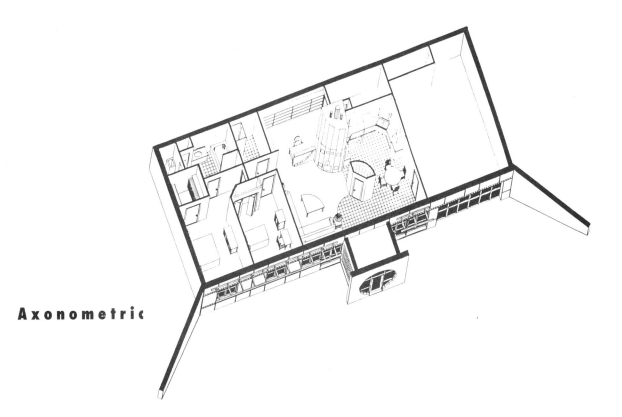

Perspective

TERRA FIRMA

Jury Comments

Contextually fit to a rural landscape. Varied forms evoke the metaphor of the farm. Technically well conceived.

A highly energy-efficient home can be spatially beautiful, moderately priced, and easy to maintain.

Given a hypothetical site in Vermont, the most energy- and cost-saving design strategy is to build a highly insulating shell. In this project we achieve an R-value of 40 in the walls and 60 in the roof. A continuous air/vapor barrier increases heat retention, prevents drafts, and creates an environment where air quality can be controlled. A fan draws fresh air into second-floor closets, where it interflows with ambient air to reduce cold drafts before being ducted into bedrooms and living spaces. Fans in kitchen and bathroom provide air exhaust. The system maintains slight positive air pressure, which helps keep external toxins out of the home environment.

The plan of the home provides optimum solar gain and generous daylight. Low-occupancy spaces, such as the stair, mudroom, and bathroom, are to the north. All living spaces and bedrooms have southern exposure. The living room, with its concrete slab floor, angles slightly to the east, to benefit from early-morning solar gain and to reduce overheating in the afternoons.

Firewood is a readily available, inexpensive, local, renewable source of fuel in Vermont. Superinsulation makes it possible to heat this house throughout most of the year with a small wood stove. The stair, serving as a plenum, and the fresh-air system move the heated air throughout the building. This convective space planning requires only a single, high-output, backup space heater.

Terra Firma

Technical Data

Gross Square Feet:
1,124

Location:
A level site in Vermont with southern exposure; suitable for most northern regions

Type:
Wood frame

Materials:
Locally milled lumber, engineered wood structural members, recycled cellulose insulation, stress-skin floor assemblies

Estimated Cost to Build:
$90,000

Estimated Cost to Heat/Cool:
$400 per year

Floor Plans and Section

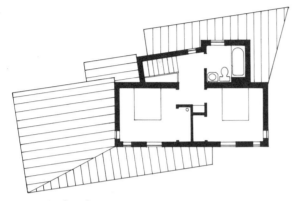

Second Floor

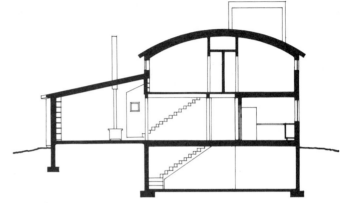

Section

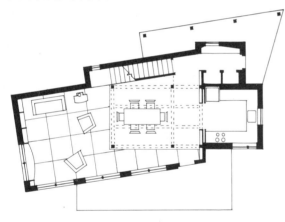

First Floor

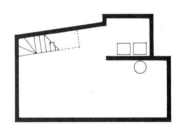

Basement

Elevations

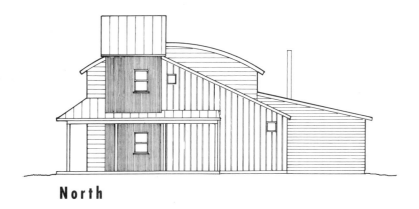

North

West

South

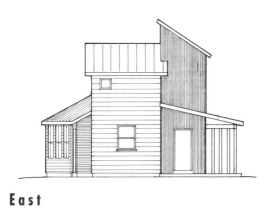

East

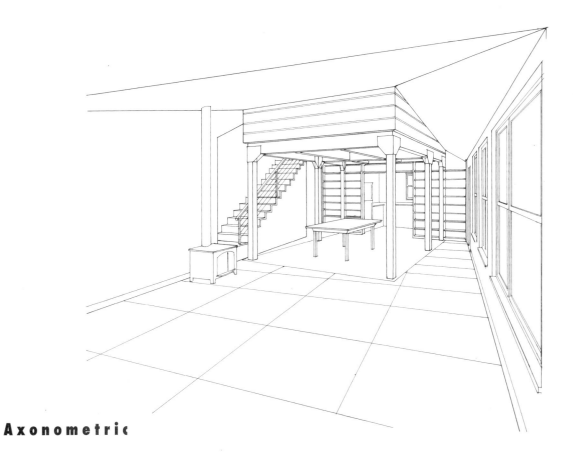

Axonometric

Perspective

WILLIAMS

First Prize

An outstanding small home infill solution in an urban setting. In this case "home" becomes an elegant urban fortress with practical, complex, and aesthetically pleasing features. A model for other challenging sites.

A crack in a well-worn city facade on a traffic-heavy road reveals previously unseen qualities. One of many forgotten gaps from the London Blitz, it still awaits occupation. Two walls of its boundary buildings tentatively cradle the site, which still bears scars from its previous use. Cracks and fissures create an opportunity for new occupation and the house "sprouts" in its forgotten cleft.

Completing a new street facade, the house answers the challenge of the aggressive road on which it sits by enfolding its occupants in a protective layer of books, buffering them from the inner-city noise outside. The south side is a stepped bookcase, or bookstep, forming a tiered living area that encourages appropriation (with sofa, work surface, etc.). On the north, the house grows towards the fresher air and quieter environment of Hoxton Square.

Climbing from the street up a flight of exposed and weathered Corten steel steps, one enters the body of the house. Concrete structural spines, which announce the route through the house as well as its eventual destination, act as plumb lines gauging the eccentricities of the site — a measuring device. The smaller interior rooms are lightly held by the larger stepped space of the bookcase room. The interior gently unfolds ahead: one inhabits, accumulates, mediates; rising at last to the perch, the widest shelf at the highest point of the bookcase room.

The house fractures away from its boundary to allow light to penetrate deep into the interior, and a rectangular light scoop lined with etched glass pierces the roof so that light runs down alongside the service core and top bedroom.

Megan Williams

Gross Square Feet:
1,250

Location:
London, England

Type:
Townhouse

Materials:
Concrete, wood, glass

Estimated Cost to Build:
$200,000

Estimated Cost to Heat/Cool:
N/A

Floor Plans

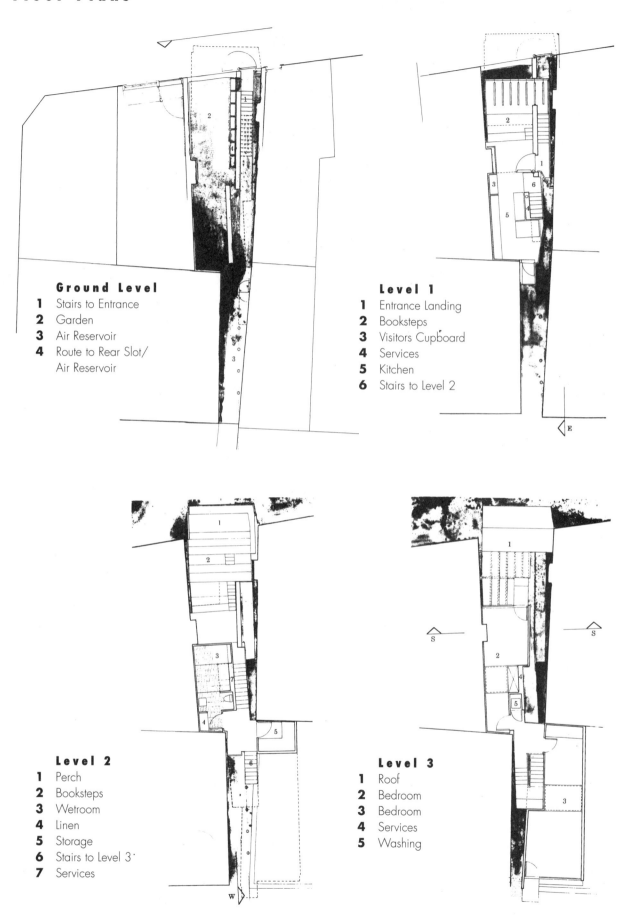

Ground Level
1. Stairs to Entrance
2. Garden
3. Air Reservoir
4. Route to Rear Slot/
   Air Reservoir

Level 1
1. Entrance Landing
2. Booksteps
3. Visitors Cupboard
4. Services
5. Kitchen
6. Stairs to Level 2

Level 2
1. Perch
2. Booksteps
3. Wetroom
4. Linen
5. Storage
6. Stairs to Level 3
7. Services

Level 3
1. Roof
2. Bedroom
3. Bedroom
4. Services
5. Washing

Interior Perspective

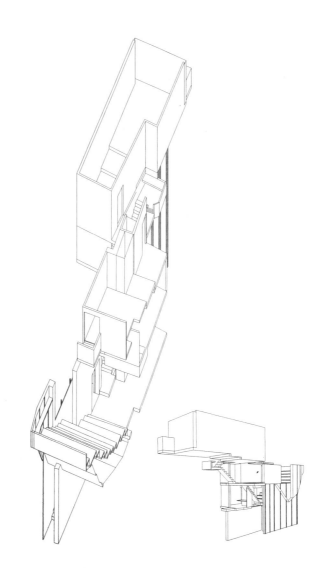

Axonometrics

Overhead Perspective

TAKITA

Second Prize

Perhaps a design for the future. A deliberate break from traditional concepts of house design to explore a variety of ways to give the illusion of greater space. The elevations deliver a special dynamic to the small house concept.

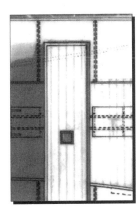

Every surface appears to be fading away in this design, leaving behind a world of silence and a feeling of utter solitude. A chilly grayness lies at the innermost heart of Japanese space. In the smoky light that pervades a Zen temple or tiny tea house, the human eye is engaged indirectly as if by stealth.

These whitened and emptied qualities of light must have been created by and for a human spirit ready to go beyond the outer aspects of things, and beyond a reality aimed to satisfy vision. Their tones express a taste for something deeper and more mysterious than traditional housing.

The structure is cable and steel. The roof is a galvanized steel sheet, and the flooring is of Japanese cedar and oak as well as exposed concrete. Landscaping includes gravel, a pond, bamboo, and maple trees.

Hideyuki Takita

Technical Data

Gross Square Feet:
1,200

Location:
Japan

Type:
Steel and cable
structure

Materials:
Steel, glass, wood

**Estimated Cost
to Build:**
$79,000

**Estimated Cost to
Heat/Cool:**
N/A

Elevations

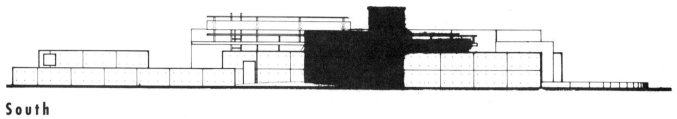

South

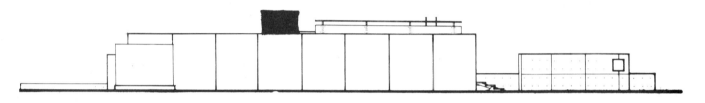

North

West

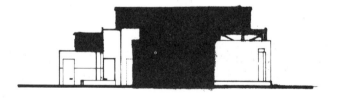

East

Floor Plan

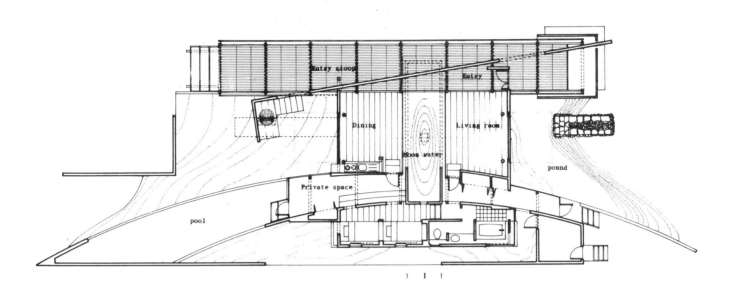

Section

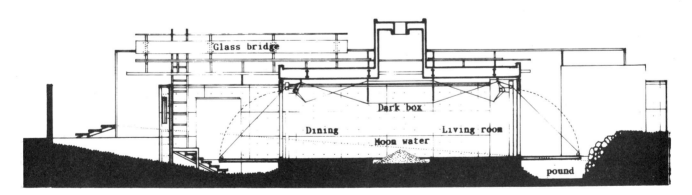

Perspective

FAYEL

Third Prize

One of the better-conceived concepts for a small house. An elevated house with a separate overhead roof, stairway, and sunscreen system. The roof contains photovoltaic cells that transfer solar energy to a nodule beneath the deck.

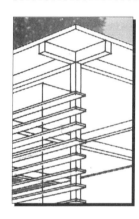

This house can be built virtually anywhere. It is designed to be constructed in a factory with manufactured materials, primarily steel for the structure and aluminum for the external skin. The roof consists of photovoltaic (PV) cell panels, so that the house can produce all of its electricity, including what it needs for heating and cooling. Although this system increases the initial cost of the house, it will pay for itself in zero energy costs over the years.

Inside, the design integrates furniture and architecture to optimize the use of space. Multipurpose spaces surround a central, concentrated block of specialized spaces. Windows allow for ample natural light to enter.

Wherever the house is built, it rests lightly on the site, seems removable, yet still protects its inhabitants against the forces of nature (by, for example, elevating the first floor and incorporating a sunscreen system on the terrace).

Christophe Fayel

Technical Data

Gross Square Feet:
1,080

Location:
France, but not site specific

Type:
Factory-built

Materials:
Steel, aluminum, wood, gypsum blocks, concrete

Estimated Cost to Build:
$250,000

Estimated Cost to Heat/Cool:
$0

Elevations

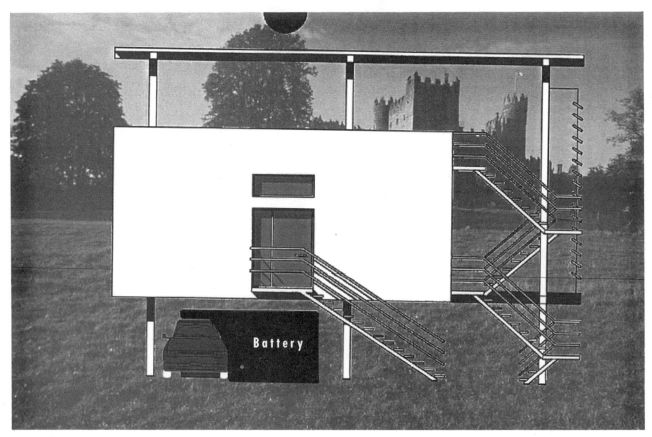

North

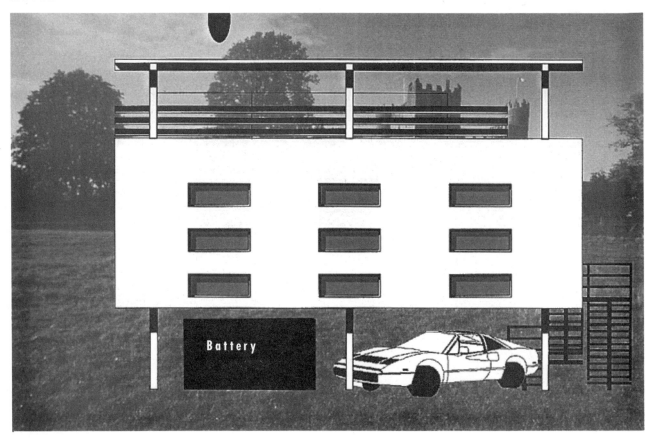

East

South

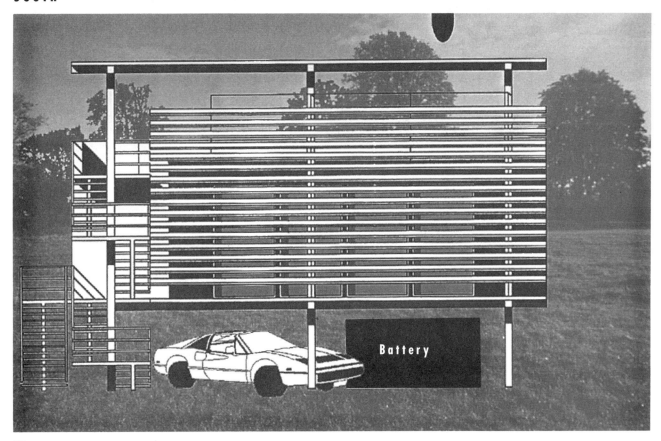

West

Floor Plans

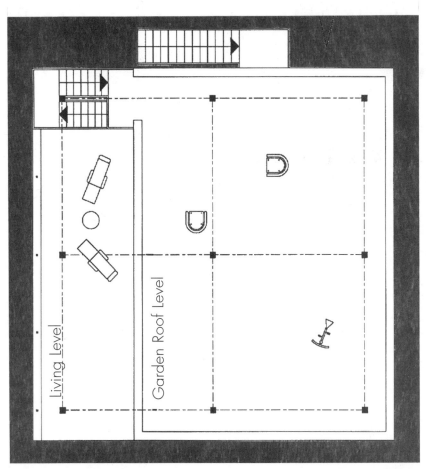

Second Floor

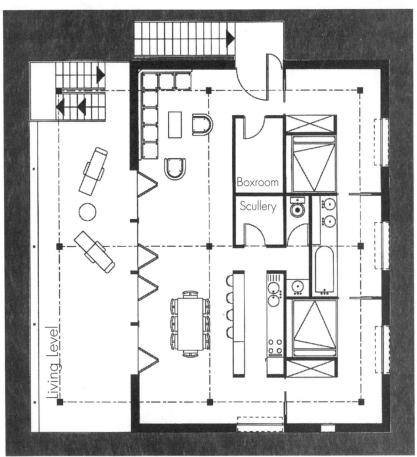

First Floor

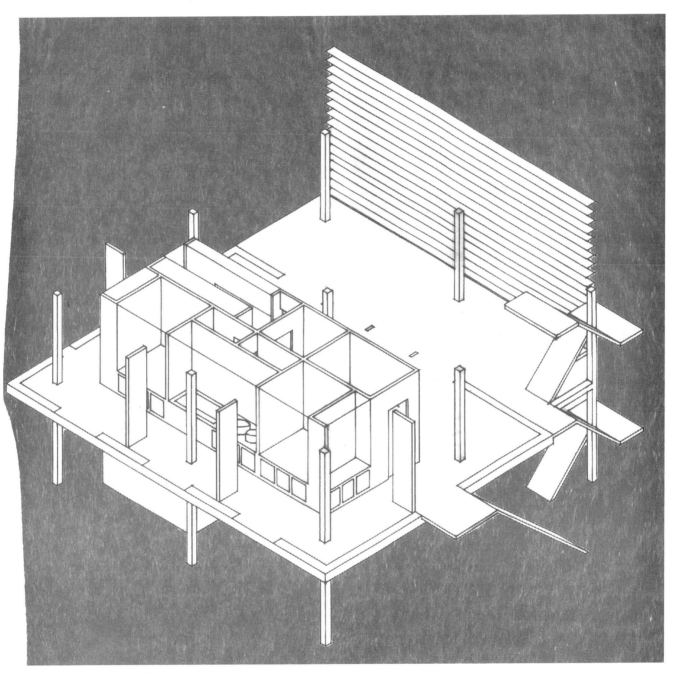

Axonometric

SPECIAL
SELECTIONS

The twenty-one designs included in this gallery were cited by the contest judges as innovative and foward looking.

Graham Smith and Tina Dhillon, Canada

Harvey Ferrero, USA

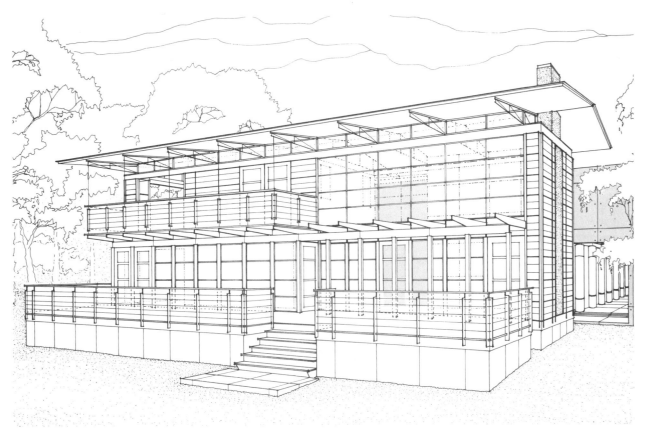

Antonio S. Gomes, USA

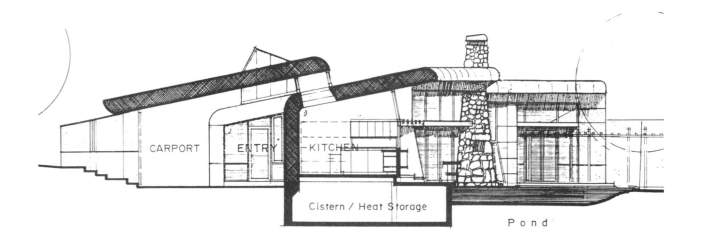

CARPORT   ENTRY   KITCHEN

Cistern / Heat Storage

Pond

Frank Alfred Hamilton, Canada

Hammond and Green Architects, Australia

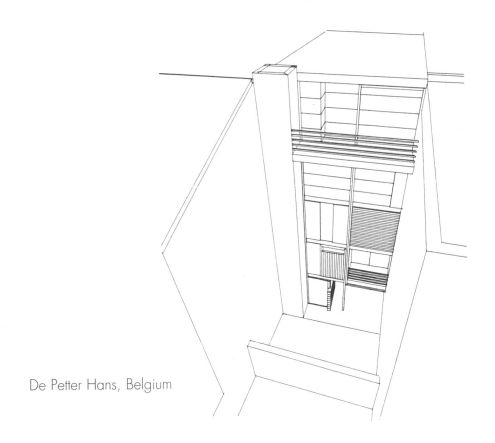

De Petter Hans, Belgium

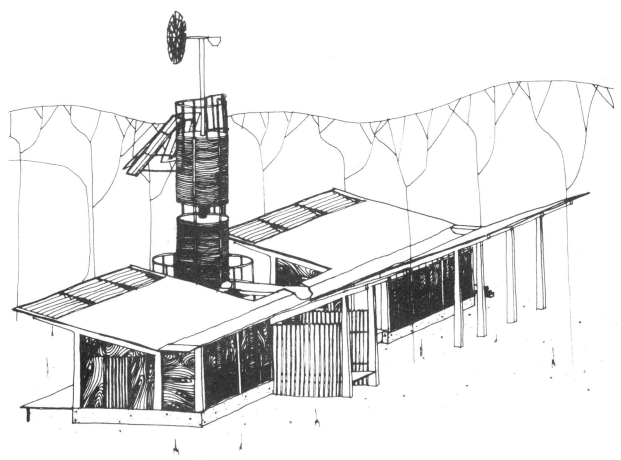

Tina Shum and Toby Wong, Australia

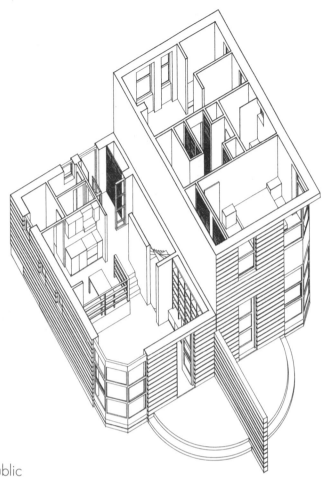

Jan Stipek, Czech Republic

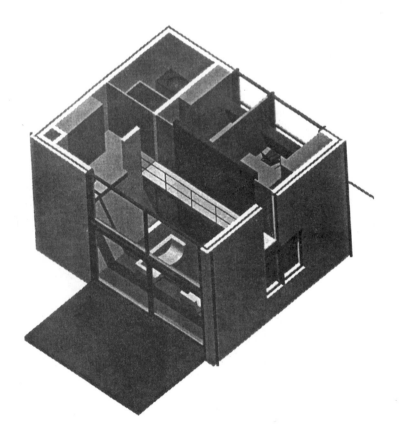

Alain Berteau and Patrick Verougstraete, Belgium

John B. Wald, USA

Anna Kemble Welch and Martin Hanley, New Zealand

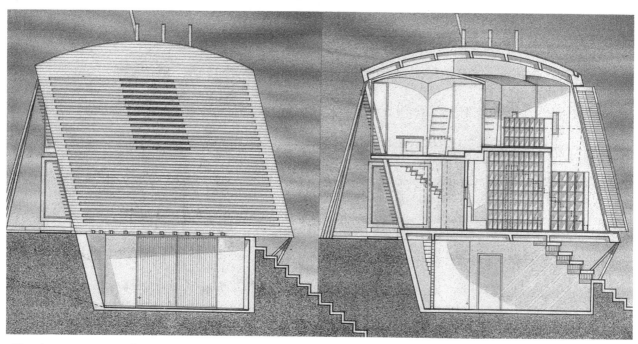

Claudio Zanirato, Italy

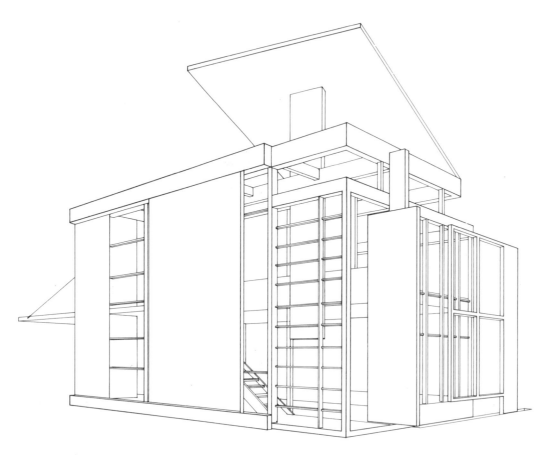

Madeleine Sanchez, USA

Todd Alan Sarantopulos, USA

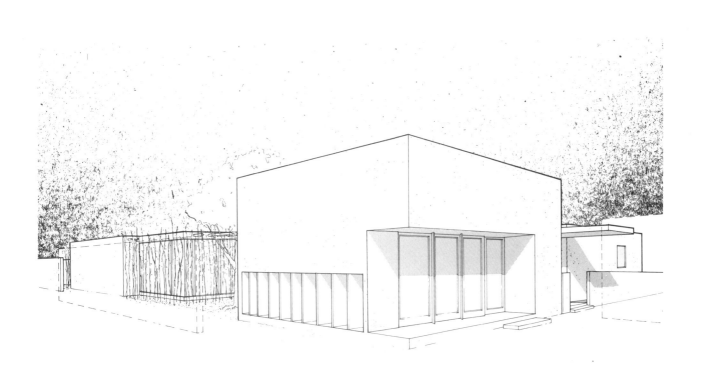

Sheng and Lesser Studio, USA

Stephane Jacq, France

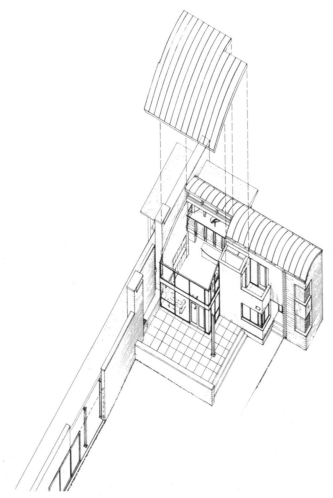

Craig King, USA

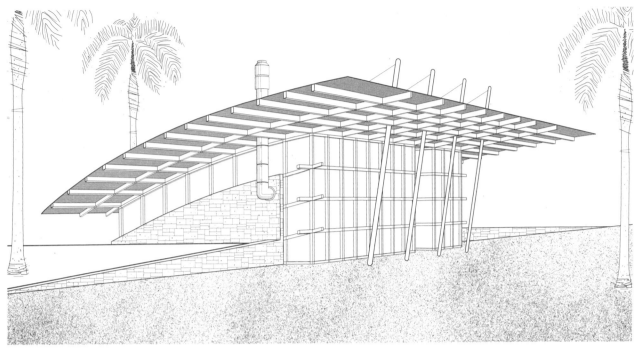

Dave Madigan, USA

PERSPECTIVE OF THE PROPOSED EXTERIOR - WINTER LAYOUT

Radu Molnar and Pascal Piccinato, France

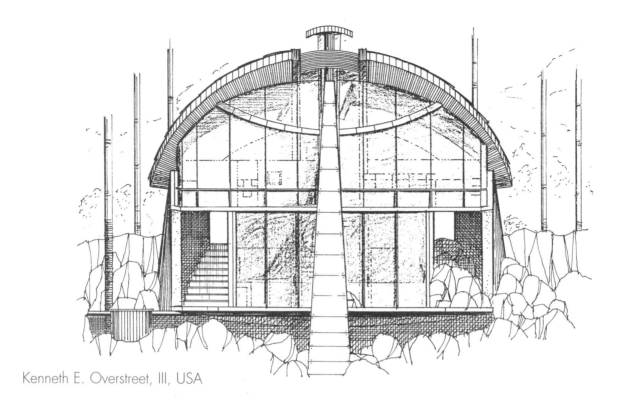

Kenneth E. Overstreet, III, USA

João Branco Pedro and José Pinto Duarte, Portugal

FOR FURTHER INFORMATION

For further information on any of the plans featured in this book, you should contact the appropriate architect or designer directly using the addresses below. Fees for working drawings and specifications will vary. The publisher, Storey Communications, Inc., assumes no financial interest in, or responsibility for, the work of the individuals selected in this design competition. If you are unable to reach any architect or designer at the printed address, please write to:

Kenneth R. Tremblay, Jr.
and Lawrence Von Bamford
Design, Merchandising,
and Consumer Sciences
Colorado State University
Fort Collins, CO 80523

Addresses

Nigel A. Holloway
5 Forest Road
Paddock Wood
Kent TN12 6JU
UK

Michael W. Folonis
Michael W. Folonis and
Associates
1731 Ocean Park
Boulevard
Santa Monica, CA 90405

Hasan Akkurt
Akkurt + Akkurt Design
1814 Duff Avenue
Ames, IA 50010

Reed M. Axelrod
Reed Axelrod Architects
2016 Walnut Street
Philadelphia, PA 19103

Christopher Blake
CBDESIGN
50 Chester Street
Allston, MA 02134

William H. Boehm
369 Congress Street,
8th Floor
Boston, MA 02210

James M. Corkill
3919 Waverly Drive
Norman, OK 73172

James F. Finigan
Five Lewis Road 1
Winchester, MA 01890

Jeffrey Fleming
Ben Allers Architects
543 28th Street
Des Moines, IA 50312

Kenneth E. King
K Architecture
568 Beatty Street
Vancouver, B.C.
Canada V6B 2L3

Remus S. L. Tsang
33 Young Street East
Waterloo, Ontario
Canada N2J 2L4

Andy Verhiel
Architects Institute of BC
28-1376 Bute Street
Vancouver, B.C.
Canada V6E 2A6

Eric Wagner
27 63rd Street, 2nd Floor
West New York, NJ
07093

Tom Leytham
TBLA
50 State Street
Montpelier, VT 05602

Lillian Mei Ngan Mah
Mnemosyne Architecture
7688 Ontario Street
Vancouver, B.C.
Canada V5X 3C5

Michael Noble
125–1857 W. 4th Avenue
Vancouver, B.C.
Canada V6J 1M4

Olgierd Miloszewicz
Oldi Constructions
71-073 Szczecin
Ul. Ku Sloncu 23
Poland

W. I. Shipley
21 Zamia Road
Gooseberry Hill
Western Australia 6076
Australia

Robert Takken
School of Architecture
Queensland Univ. of
   Technology
2 George Street
Queensland 4005
Australia

Giulio Fabbri
Via Sammartina 12 —
44040 Chiesuol Del
   Fosso Ferrera
Italy

Carlo Giuliani
Studio Architetto Carlo
   Giuliani
Dorsoduro 623 —
30123 Venezia
Italy

Ulrik Hellum
Eidsten
3267 Larvik
Norway

Mark and Linda Keane
Studio 1032 Architecture
3541 N. Hackett
Shorewood, WI 53211

Mark B. Luther
School of Architecture and
   Building
Deakin University
Geelong
Victoria 3217
Australia

Studio of Pacific
   Architecture
2nd Floor
Hibernian House
   89 Willis Street
PO Box 11517
Wellington
New Zealand

Don Buoen
1520 South Evanston
Tulsa, OK 74104

Daniel L. Faoro
Department of Architecture
North Dakota State
   Univerity
P.O. Box 5285
Fargo, ND 58105

Jawaid Haider
School of Architecture
Pennsylvania State
   University
178 W. Hamilton Avenue
State College, PA 16801

Bruce Shindelus
25487 Buckly Drive
Murrieta, CA 92563

Synthesis Architects
P.O. Box 383
Schenectady, NY 12301

Terra Firma
RR1 Box 371A
Randolph Center, VT
   05061

Megan Williams
2 Grenville Road
London N19 4EH
UK

Hideyuki Takita
Institute of Engineering —
   Architecture
Kanto Gakuin University
4834 Mutsuura-chyo
   Kanazawa-ku
Yokohama 236
Japan

Christophe Fayel
15, Rue de la Grande
   Armee
13001 Marseille
France